The Kids Guide To Business

Jeff M. Brown

Please see our web site at www.TheKidsGuideToBusiness.com for additional activities and opportunities for kids

Proceeds from this book are being used to further develop the social venture of www.teachingkidsbusiness.com and www.kidse-marketplace.com. Proceeds will help provide kids with programming and opportunities to learn about business.

TeachingKidsBusines

I

Written by: Jeff M. Brown, Founder of TeachingKidsBusiness.com and Kidse-Marketplace.com

Published by TeachingKidsBusiness.com.

Proceeds from this book are being used to further develop the social venture of www.teachingkidsbusiness.com and www.kidse-marketplace.com. Proceeds will help provide kids with programming and opportunities to learn about business.

Paperback 1st Edition

ISBN 0-9733058-1-9

UPC 806494000652

Revised March 12, 2004

Visit our web site at www.TheKidsGuideToBusiness.com for additional activities and opportunities for kids.

Introduction

Let's start with the thought that "business is a game kids can play." Let's treat business as a game and have some fun with it. You can play around with developing product ideas, think how your business can compete with others, how you can win customers and get people interested in your business. There is lots of information in this book so use as much or as little as you want to play around with business.

To make business as much fun as possible for kids, we encourage kids to create the fun in business. As kids learn to develop a business and make many business decisions, it is their choice on how much fun is involved.

This is a guide to help kids get started in business by providing them with a framework to explore business. Some kids will use this book as a reference to develop their own businesses and others will use it as an introduction to business. There can be immediate results (do business now) or the start of a long thinking, exploration and discovery process.

This book was inspired by hundreds of kid's résumés reviewed by TeachingKidsBusiness.com. TeachingKidsBusiness.com realized that kids do not have a lot of work experiences or business opportunities beyond household chores (i.e. dishwashing, putting out the garbage, cleaning their rooms, walking and caring for pets). We believe that kids are capable of much more and are ready for the challenge.

We have provided a very detailed table of contents to allow you to jump around and explore the different sections in the book. The introductory sections should be used to ease you into business, or you can jump ahead to the DAB section where kids can start to Develop A Business (DAB). We have also added programming through our web site at www.TheKidsGuideToBusiness.com and a Kids Business Rewards Program™.

We use the term "business" to cover the commercial activities of companies and career choices. We believe that as you prepare for business, you are also preparing for a career in business. We would like kids to think of going into business and choosing a career as two things with similar goals requiring similar preparation. Business is where your career happens. This book will help kids prepare for careers and explore business opportunities. Learning to develop a business will help kids learn to work in a business.

This book is geared for kids 8-18 years of age and aims to make kids feel confident in developing their own business. It is written in a way that will help you understand business better by discussing business basics in a kid-friendly way. This reading experience will provide ideas, encourage, empower, challenge and provide an excellent learning experience, while taking kids through an approach to developing a business.

Since business is new to many kids, this book demonstrates how to explore business and how adults can use this book to help kids learn about business. Our A to Z approach is really an introduction to business through the development of a business.

The Kids' Guide To Business provides a very unique approach by helping kids understand about business and also encourages adults to take an active role in this. Once we introduce kids to business, we will have given their future a jumpstart. Naturally, this will spark a kid's interest and they will start asking questions, exploring and experimenting in business, which will help them prepare for their eventual future/career in business.

References have been made to the business case of the lemonade stand to show kids about business in a fun and relevant way. Kids will learn about business by applying business basics to the lemonade stand example. We believe that all kids understand the lemonade stand business and will feel comfortable applying even sophisticated business practices to this simple example. Kids may not actually operate a lemonade stand business and it's not important that they do, but this approach will allow kids to use their imaginations in developing their businesses keeping the lemonade stand business in mind. Many kids will think in terms of the lemonade stand example and then actually apply the concepts to their business idea.

TeachingKidsBusiness.com's "Develop A Business" or DAB approach takes kids through the many steps that are used to develop a business. In the DAB approach, we introduce business terms through a two-step process. First, we define the business term and then we explain it. Secondly, we apply the term to a lemonade stand business to make the ideas and concepts simple, fun and easy to understand. Kids can then apply this to other businesses.

This book has been developed to enhance the programming of www.teachingkidsbusiness.com as proceeds from this book will be used to further develop this social venture and create more business learning, experiences and opportunities for kids. In addition, kids will have the opportunity to apply their business skills in www.kidse-marketplace.com. Let's learn about business while we discuss and develop a lemonade stand business! Let's "plan a stand"! Let's develop a business!

Acknowledgements

The important concept behind this book is to get kids involved in business and to provide kids with business experience. This has been accomplished in a number of ways and the momentum is growing.

I would like to thank Amey Harding, Tyler Brown and Hayley Brown for their editing, perspectives and idea generation support. They have been very instrumental throughout the development of TeachingKidsBusiness.com and The Kids' Guide To Business.

A special thank you to Hayley Brown for her cover design and kid-friendly advice.

Thank you to the hundreds of kids who have shared their résumés with us on www.teachingkidsbusiness.com and provided their perspectives on how they plan to prepare for their future. By looking at the résumés it became clear to us that kids have career & business ambitions at an early age but they need help and experience to obtain their goals.

I am fortunate to have had access to the talents of many kids through our www.teachingkidsbusiness.com/jobs-for-kids.htm program. Kids reviewed our book and provided valuable comments.

Many kids have also offered their comments on the concept of teaching kids business.

I was fortunate to have received a résumé from Ida Wong, a recent Ryerson Journalism graduate. Ida was given the opportunity to edit the book and provided very impressive editing expertise while developing her skills and gaining experience.

Thank you to the many people who have supported the social venture of TeachingKidsBusiness.com. The compliments, encouragement, comments and programming input have helped create unique opportunities for kids. I would like to thank Tara Sorensen for her support in the initial development of the TeachingKidsBusiness.com web site.

Thank you for buying this book and supporting our teaching kids business initiative. The proceeds from this book will help us grow as a business, demonstrate business to kids and expand our programming to impact the future of kids.

Thank you in advance for taking the time and interest to teach kids business. By taking an interest in this subject matter you will gain from the wonderful opportunities this book has to offer and from business in general.

It really does take a community to educate a child. I encourage you to share information with us to further develop the subject of this book and TeachingKidsBusiness.com. See our community involvement section @ www.teachingkidsbusiness.com. Thank you for being part of our community.

Jeff M. Brown

About the Author

Jeff M. Brown, B.A., CMA, an entrepreneur, businessperson, Certified Management Accountant, Internet publisher, parent and individual who cares about the future of kids. His personal experiences and his 30 years in business have influenced the development of a very original and effective approach to teaching kids business.

As a parent, Jeff recognizes the importance of preparing kids for independence and a future in business. Jeff is a big believer in nurturing and empowering kids in a positive way at an early age. He believes kids have tremendous potential and are only constrained by the resources and support we give them.

Like most working people, Jeff has made several career changes. These experiences have helped Jeff better understand the need for people to identify their strengths, weaknesses and interests to help them prepare and evolve their careers in business.

Jeff believes we should offer kids business related experiences at an early age. This exposure will help kids shape their attitudes and explore possibilities while engaging and exciting them about business and their future.

Through the social venture www.TeachingKidsBusiness.com, Jeff's mission is to help prepare kids for a successful business future. TeachingKidsBusiness.com's web site has reached thousands of kids worldwide and is contributing to a growing awareness of the potential of kids in business.

He is actively developing www.kidse-marketplace.com to give kids opportunities to apply what they have learned from this book. He has written numerous editorials on the subject of teaching kids business, which are available at www.teachingkidsbusiness.com.

Jeff is very committed and passionate about teaching kids business and will continue to publish. This is his first book.

Kids' Guide To Business
Table Of Contents

Chapter 1

Kid's Introduction

In This Chapter

Overview For Kids
The Fun Side Of Business
What This Book Can Do For You

Overview For Kids

We hope this book is a launching pad for you to start exploring and preparing yourself for business. If Harry Potter can get kids reading, let's use The Kids' Guide To Business to get kids interested in business.

Basically, we want you to take on the challenge of participating in a great business experience. You can do this on paper (think, draw or plan it out) or actually develop and run a lemonade stand business or any other business you desire.

We know you can master business and this will be a good chance for you to take charge, give it a try and prove it. You will become the decision maker as we give you lots of tips on things you should consider while developing your business. Consider yourself the President of your new business venture. You are empowered to run the business the way you think it should be run, by actually running it or imagining how to run it.

We have called this book a "guide to business" as we believe it will help guide you into and through business. Our approach is to discuss business with you by referencing a lemonade stand business. You can apply this guide to any business you may be considering. The unique thing about this book is that you can understand & learn about business and gain business experience and not even set-up a lemonade stand.

You will surprise yourself on how simple it is to develop a business when you know what steps to take. If you are new to business, we have lots of tips to help you learn. If you feel you are a little too old to actually run a lemonade stand, then give the "plan a stand" a chance. If you don't want to run a business yet, write and draw out how you would like to run your business in the future.

You can "plan a business" as a class, a business club, with friends, family or on your own. There are lots of challenges and lots to be learned from this experience. Planning is using your imagination to see what you would do before you actually do it.

Business is everything from what your parents and others do to earn money, what stores are doing and where you buy things. Business is about people earning money to have the things they need (food, house, car, clothes) and to have the things they want or to do the things they want to do (sports, entertainment, travel, etc.).

Business is what people usually do after they finish going to school. School helps you develop many of the basic skills you need in business. Business includes terms like working, career, job, occupation, stores, factories, restaurants, and activities outside of your family and school.

Business can also be looked at as how things work around you. When we talk about business and preparing for business, it can be as simple as being aware of stores that you walk into or companies that you see on TV. You can learn a lot about business by asking yourself simple questions like "How do they do this?", "How well do they do this?" and "How could I do this?"

This is really about spending some time on your future - investing time in you! At some point in the future you will spend more and more of your time involved in business or working a job. If you could spend more time preparing yourself, you will have a better chance of succeeding in business.

Your future career may be one of the many business job responsibilities that you will encounter in this book. Your lemonade stand business might be the opportunity for you to discover your talents and develop your business skills. Are you good at making things (design), selling things (sales person), creating advertisements (advertising professional), keeping track of money (accounting), telling people about your product & business (marketing) or organizing the business (managing) - give it a try and find out! You may even make the best lemonade in the world!

2

Take the time to further explore the different jobs available in business. Once you have found an area of business that interests you, try and understand the skills that are required, how to prepare for that career and develop a plan for you to get the needed skills.

Take some additional time to explore online links at www.TheKidsGuideToBusiness.com for hundreds of additional pages of business resources and experiences. Keep your purchase receipt for this book, as it is your ticket to other programs.

Create a business card and show it to your friends, just as if you were showing them your latest toy, telling them about the newest song or describing a video game or a new movie you just saw. Tell them about the business you are developing and all the neat experiences you are having. Tell them you are going to be a business star instead of talking about other people who are stars (i.e. Sports stars, movie stars and singers).

We could add gimmicks to make our book more fun, but we would rather have you create fun while doing business. We provide you with a framework to do business and it's up to you to make it fun by using your imagination. As you develop a business, you are in charge of the business, which includes the fun. At some point, share with us how you had fun with business and we will write another book on the Fun with Business™.

Invest time in yourself while you explore business. Have a great experience in whatever you choose in your future. Just remember - you get out of life what you put into it. If you work hard at something and put a lot into it, you will get a lot out of it – from rewards to experience and satisfaction.

We hope this is an opportunity for you to try business and feel the pride when you sit back and say, "I did it!"

Use this book as a project to help you learn about business, discover your talents, challenge yourself in new ways and have some fun. Enjoy discussing business with your friends, family and at school. Dream a little, dream big and go after your dreams… starting now!

Good luck in business!

The Fun Side of Business™

While business may not appear to be as exciting as an action video game or a big sports event, business is something that **you** can make as exciting and as challenging as you want. At first, you are probably thinking that business is boring. It's not! Being in business is like playing a game. You make it as fun as you want it to be.

Fun is a big challenge in business. I am going to take you through a lot of good learning material, but like most business writers I kind of forgot about fun. I had so much that I wanted to tell you that I just started writing and writing about business stuff in a kid-friendly way. Most businesses forget that having fun is important. I know how important fun is for kids since kids tell me all the time. I know in all my business experiences and all the research I do on businesses, I can't find as much as I would like about the fun side of business. I try to write in a fun way, but I know that I need some help. I thought about rewriting the book after already writing and rewriting it many times, until I figured out how to make business really fun – by letting kids make business fun!

In this book, I create business experiences for kids. Kids take on the responsibility of learning about and developing a business. Therefore, the responsibility or the job of making business fun has been delegated to you. As you begin to develop your business, you are asked to create the job of "Vice President of Fun" to ensure your business experience is fun. I encourage kids to be in charge of the businesses they develop, the amount of fun they have and others around them have. Let kids determine how much fun they need, how to create more fun and how it contributes to the success of a business. Most importantly, you should learn how to balance fun with a successful business.

Kids, throughout this book I would like you to think, "How can I make this fun?" The amount of fun you think about is only limited by your imagination. The amount of fun you actually have with your business experience is your choice.

Please help me bring kids into business and bring out the fun side of business!

"Business is a game kids can make fun!"
Jeff Brown, Author of "The Kids' Guide To Business"

How Kids Can Approach Business

Business is really a new territory for you to explore and so it becomes a new challenge. It is a new game that you can learn to play. Once you catch on to business you can be assured that business will respond by creating more business related products and opportunities. As you and many more kids get interested in business, it could become the next kids' phenomena.

The approach we would like you to take with this book is similar in preparing for a pro athlete career. Kids dream about playing in the pro leagues, they watch and learn about the sport, they read about it, they practice when they have time and they play in leagues and pick-up games to improve. Parents also spend a lot of time and money on travel, equipment, lessons, coaching etc. What if you spend a little time on preparing yourself for business, like you would for sports? Don't you think it would help you make the "pro leagues of business?" Just try and manage business preparation the way kids are managed in sports.

You are basically a kid for about 20 years and work for 40 to 45 years. In your first 20 years, have lots of fun, but spend some time learning about business to help you through your working years. We are **not** talking about dropping your favourite sport and spending all your time on business preparation. We are suggesting that you start thinking about business, ask questions, observe what people do and try to understand what you would like to do, what you may be good at doing and how to prepare yourself.

It is important that you try hard at school and learn as much as you can. Realize school provides you with a very broad education and not necessarily the preparation for a particular career. The accomplishments of finishing high school, college or university will not guarantee you a successful career in business. It is your responsibility to plan your education, choose your career path and understand the necessary skills, additional education, training and experience you will need.

Find a little time to start exploring business and preparing for your future.

What This Book Can Do For You

You never know where this business experience will take you!

This book will provide you with lots of information and good ideas to help you out. This book alone will not make things happen, as it is up to you to do something with the information. This book will help you understand business and develop a business, but you will have to take the next steps to make it happen.

Any experience that you have will be very impactful and if managed properly can have a very positive influence on your future. We hope to create awareness and positive business experiences at an early age to help set the foundation to shape your successful business future.

If we can spark an interest in business, then you will ask questions and begin to figure things out as you go through life. You don't have to wait till college to learn about business. By starting now, you will do something good for yourself.

We realize that kids are people with tremendous amounts of potential and often their full potential is not reached if they are not given the tools, opportunities and support to do so. A book can be a wonderful way to reach out to kids in new ways and provide access to ideas that will help them reach their potential. We hope that this book will help you to understand and reach your potential.

This book can help you:

- Explore business in a fun and interesting way
- Introduce you to business
- Prepare for business
- Launch into business
- Develop business skills
- Understand your talents and interests
- Begin healthy conversations and observations about business

This book is also a business investment in you that provides opportunities for you to gain valuable experience. Take the time to explore business further through the book updates and links available to you at www.TheKidsGuideToBusiness.com.

Kids, this is a good point to skip ahead to "The Business Case Of Little Johnny And The Lemonade Stand" – Chapter 4. You are welcome to read through the next few sections or come back to them in the future. You are probably anxious to learn more about business and how to develop a business, so feel free to jump ahead now.

Lets get started!

Chapter 2

Adult's Introduction

In This Chapter

Adult Overview
Our Unique Approach To Teaching Kids Business
Why We Chose The Title – The Kids' Guide To Business
How Parents Can Engage Kids In Business
An Approach For Teachers To Teach Kids Business

Adult Overview

"Business, a game kids can play™!"
Jeff Brown, Founder of TeachingKidsBusiness.com

We would like kids to think of business as a game that requires skills, talents, practice, rules, teams, competitions, winners and losers. The fact that business is a good challenge for kids makes it a fun experience like many other games they play.

This is a book that helps kids figure out how to "develop a business" (DAB). We hope to get kids thinking about business, give them a business framework to work with, create confidence and opportunities for them.

This book has been created to be a "kids' guide to business", in other words a business program geared specifically towards kids. There are many "how-to guides" on the market, but we are trying to approach it differently for kids. We introduce business terms, discuss them and then apply them to a lemonade stand business. Kids are provided with questions and ideas to consider as they apply business concepts to the development of their own business.

This book was inspired by the view that kids have tremendous potential and when we give them the proper tools, opportunities and encouragement, they will accomplish many great things, including business. We feel that kids are interested in business and if we connect with them with terms and examples they can relate to, we will provide a good experience for them.

If kids took some of their time, for example, one half hour a week which they would normally spend surfing the Internet, talking on the phone or watching TV, and use it to dream and prepare for their future - they would all be better off.

This book has been developed to help kids step into the business world. We have made it easier for kids to learn and develop a business using a step-by step approach. We know the concept of developing a business could be overwhelming but we have broken the process down into simple manageable steps.

The use of a lemonade stand is an ideal business case because it is an excellent example that kids can relate to. The steps you take to develop a business are the same steps we take kids through in developing a lemonade stand. Once kids can develop a lemonade stand using our DAB approach, they can apply it to many other business opportunities.

We need to start offering more of what is good for kids, rather then what they want or may be use to. It is kind of like junk food. Kids love junk food but it is not the smart choice and can lead to lots of health problems. Business may not be a top choice for kids but it is a smart choice for their future.

TeachingKidsBusiness.com has found research indicating kids have fun when it satisfies emotional needs. Kids will have fun as their needs for challenge, respect, control, power, accomplishment, knowledge, participation, safety, pride, acceptance, success, and nurturing are satisfied throughout the book.

Our research also tells us kids want learning to be fun and we realize that this is a crucial element for kids. Like school, business can be fun, but unfortunately there are times when it is not. As kids evolve in business they will learn that fun is only one of many rewards.

Our planning approach of a lemonade stand business attracts participation from a wider age group. The image of a lemonade stand is usually associated with kids 5-10 years old. The exercise of planning a business can engage older kids and more kids in general. This also allows younger kids to feel that they are actually running a "big business" or a real business. Kids from early elementary school to college level can enjoy and be challenged by the DAB planning framework in this book. We believe the 9-14 age group will be the main users of the book.

When we ask the question of how much you should sell your lemonade for, kids of all ages will have an answer, but arrive at it with different insights and recommendations. They will be challenged by the question and eager to find out what the price should be or what the right answer is. Throughout the book, all age groups will be challenged by questions that arise in developing a business.

Our planning approach is also a safety precaution for children since our streets are not as safe as they used to be. Parents, a generation ago would allow their kids to sit out by the street, confident they would be safe in their neighbourhood. Now, parents are more reluctant to leave their kids unattended in their neighbourhoods and kids are much more aware and cautious about dealing with strangers.

This book takes a different approach to the usual lemonade stand business. We have created the option of an indoor business planning exercise with more writing and drawing exercises. Kids can also explore many more ideas and continue to be very creative as they plan their business on paper. The activity of planning a lemonade stand provides an impactful business experience. Kids can **pretend** to run a stand by planning and acting out the activities inside or they can actually set-up and run the stand outside.

We have also used links to online Internet programming at www.TheKidsGuideToBusiness.com and www.teachingkidsbusiness.com to provide updates and additional activities.

Our Unique Approach To Teaching Kids Business

Our approach is to talk to kids about business in a way they can understand, using language they can relate to, empowering them to develop a business and trying to bring fun to the business.

We know kids can do amazing things if they are given the tools, opportunities and support. We can begin to prepare them for business by helping them develop business skills early in life. Kids stand for potential and with the right attention and guidance they will master business at an early age and thus be better prepared for the future.

We would like to see kids participate in conversations about business. Kids should share their business experiences as they commonly share stories about an accomplishment, a special day at school, a trip to the zoo or the best parts of a movie.

Throughout the book, kids are encouraged to think and imagine their way through various business situations. We do not give them all the answers to business success, but we empower and engage them to take steps, ask questions and come up with ideas. We feel our approach will create a lasting learning experience rather than a memory exercise.

We know business preparation and experiences can be great for kids. There are many things that kids are exposed to that shape who they are and who they become. If we can create positive business experiences that build self-esteem, confidence and good character traits, we will make great contributions to the lives of kids. We believe engaging kids in business will deliver good life experiences.

We also believe kids are ready to "play the game of business" at an early age. Business is like any other game with; rules, challenges, competition and once you learn how to play the game you can win.

Kids can learn about business. Kids can do business. Kids can have fun experimenting with business. Kids can have fun exploring business. Kids can find lots of questions to ask and uncover the answers to them.

Once we believe in the capability of kids, we can proceed with patience and support to teach many wonderful things about business.

Why We Chose The Title - The Kids' Guide To Business

The book title was a difficult exercise. The problem with any title is the final choice may limit the understanding of what the book is about and what it is trying to accomplish. We have chosen a main title and included sub-titles to help communicate the scope of this book and add clarity to the title.

We think the phrase "guide to business" suggests kids who use this book will be guided into business. We realize business is not necessarily something you just jump into. We show kids the many steps that should be considered when developing a business and we give tips to adults on talking to kids about business.

Preparing And Launching Kids Into Business

The main premise of this book is to prepare kids for business. We discuss business language (business terms), provide assistance in making business decisions, demonstrate job responsibilities, develop business skills and help kids discover their talents & interests.

Kids are effectively launched into business by developing a business. We are also working to provide kids with the opportunity to launch a business in www.kidse-marketplace.com. This initiative will hopefully engage kids to go into business worldwide.

A to Z's of Business For Kids

We often see the ABC's or A to Z suggesting the basics and much more are being covered. We have chosen this phrase to suggest that we have covered many business basics. We discuss very basic business terms and apply them to more complicated and advanced business practices. We cover a broad range of topics from naming a business or product to mergers and acquisitions.

Develop A Business For Kids

We have created the DAB (develop a business) approach to help kids develop a business. DAB is a framework to empower kids to work through the development of a business. By providing kids with steps or "decisions in business", they will learn to assume responsibility and gain confidence in developing a business. Valuable experience can be gained from going through the DAB approach for a lemonade stand and then applying the framework to other business opportunities.

Applying Business Basics Using The Lemonade Stand Business Case

The lemonade stand is an excellent business case to reference business learning with kids. Kids can easily understand business terms and practices when they are being related to a lemonade stand. Many kids have operated lemonade stands, know the business and can easily relate to it.

How Parents Can Engage Kids In Business

Don't underestimate your ability to influence or teach your kids about business. Kids may not appear to take direction or listen to you, but you do have an impact. Your attitude towards topics, are usually very clear to them whether they agree or disagree with your perspective.

It is our belief adults in general do not respect kids' perspectives on business. This is demonstrated by the fact many adults avoid business conversations with kids. If adults and parents could engage kids in business related conversations, they would find this would lead to many interesting discussions.

Consider having business discussions with your kids so they develop the confidence to join or initiate business-related conversations. Kids will ask questions when they feel they are being listened to and answers will be provided.

As a parent, you should not be focussed on what career you want your child to pursue, but rather help them understand their choices, interests and talents. The best influence is to help them find something that makes sense for their needs, interests and abilities.

Please do not judge your child's business experience. At this stage in their development, successful and unsuccessful business experiences are good. The successes build confidence while the failures become great learning lessons.

This book will provide you with valuable information and a framework to start discussions on business. You can discuss business in great depths by helping your child explore our DAB section. You can relate business principles to your business experience and to other businesses that interest you and your child. You can explore business further through links to activities at www.TheKidsGuideToBusiness.com.

Be creative and make it fun to engage your child.

An Approach For Teachers To Teach Kids Business

This book was partly inspired by requests from teachers at www.teachingkidsbusiness.com for basic business programming for kids.

This book provides basic business terms and applications to introduce kids to business. We have covered a broad range of business topics and presented the information in a way that can be discussed and further explored. The book can be used for a wide range of ages as we believe younger and older kids will relate to the book differently and experience challenges at different levels.

The lemonade stand is an excellent way to have kids relate to business. Many of them have tried a lemonade stand business or seen one in operation. Take this business icon and expand the experience in your classroom and beyond.

Use this book as an introduction to business, a guide, a model or framework to which you can add elements based on the abilities of your students. You can use certain components of the book if you have a specific topic in mind. (ie. Marketing, advertising, etc.)

The numerous business decisions kids will encounter in the DAB section can be used as an introduction to career discussions. Each of the business decisions is actually a job responsibility of current career positions in many companies.

The exercise of developing a lemonade stand business integrates many components of the school curriculum. This book provides a learning framework that encourages collaboration, brainstorming, application of concepts, research, problem solving, developing of skills, presentation of ideas and making recommendations.

This book can be used as a program, a project, a fun activity, a fundraiser or a starting point for much more:

- To explore career choices
- To introduce business terms and concepts
- To teach business basics to your class
- To develop project skills

Chapter 3

Ways To Use This Book

In This Chapter

Exploration of Business
Develop A Business – DAB
Discovering & Developing Talents, Skills And Interests
Interest Reading
Fun And Social Activities
Developing Your Imagination – Putting Your Imagination To Work
Home Schooling And Tutoring
Kid's Business Club
Competition/Contest
Developing Commercial Opportunities For Kids

The subject of business is new for many kids, so we have developed some ideas for ways to get them started.

This book can be used by kids of all ages to teach business at a variety of levels (introduction to advanced). This book has been created for kids and adults who are interested in influencing the future of kids.

The experience kids gain from this book can be enhanced by using additional resources from the business programming of the www.teachingkidsbusiness.com web site. We hope our guide is the starting point for additional exploration of business. We have provided updates and activities at www.TheKidsGuideToBusiness.com

As a tool to teach kids business, this book should be used in a way that works best for the reader. There is no right or wrong way to read and reference this book, but the reader needs to choose. The reader may want to use a few sections to get started or proceed to many other business topics and opportunities.

The following are some ideas on how this book can be used and the possible outcomes you can expect:

- Kids working on their own or with the help of a parent
- A group of friends
- A youth or community group
- A kid's business club
- Teachers in a school class

Exploration of Business

Kids may not have had the opportunity to explore or think about going into business. As kids read through this book it should get them thinking about the different aspects of a business. Children will learn from this book and help jumpstart their futures.

Once kids have a grasp of the business basics, they can begin to explore so much more. As kids start to learn the basic business language and the way business works, they can proceed more easily in business. We hope to give kids the framework to look at and explore business.

This book will also refer kids to other types of business experiences in www.teachingkidsbusiness.com. Here you will be able to find hundreds of pages on business programming.

Develop A Business - DAB

Our DAB approach is like writing a fictional story about what you are going to do in business. In the story you would discuss all your ideas on running a lemonade stand. In the business world we call this business planning (writing down ideas) and like story telling, we use a certain framework to develop a business plan. The DAB section gets kids planning a business by using a fun activity.

Business planning can be used to figure things out before you invest the time and money in a business. Planning can be fun because you can imagine some great things and dream about how successful you will be.

Discovering And Developing Talents, Skills And Interests

The development of a lemonade stand business is an opportunity for kids to understand their talents, develop skills in business and identify their interests. Talents are natural abilities of learning or doing something. Skills are abilities that come from training and practice. Interests are having feelings of curiosity towards something – to excite the attention of curiosity.

Your talents will become apparent as you develop a business. You will learn and develop skills and discover your interests as you work through this book. If you show interest in a certain area of the lemonade stand experience, it will help you understand areas of business that may be better suited to you.

- If you are interested in the preparation of the lemonade, you have a love of making things
- If you enjoy talking to people and trying to sell products to them, you have a natural talent for selling
- If you are interested in preparing advertisements for the stand you have creative talent
- If you have good ideas for promotions you have a talent for the promotional business
- If you like managing money, you have a knack for math or finance

Every experience you have with the DAB activities should help you develop skills and understand your strengths, weaknesses and interests. Once you figure this out, you are well on your way to preparing yourself for business.

The secret to making sure your future jobs are a good fit for you is to understand the skills you need and how they match your interests, talents and skills. In the future, you will find you may take jobs to gain the necessary skills for your "dream job".

Interest Reading

Let's not forget this is a book for reading. We refer to this book as a guide for kids, but it is still an easy and interesting read. If it helps you understand business or helps to launch you into business, then it is an added bonus. As long as you find this book interesting with some new ideas and lasting impressions, we have reached our goal.

Business is not currently a favourite reading category for kids, but we have to start somewhere and this is a good start.

Fun And Social Activities

We have asked kids to take responsibility for developing the fun side of their business experiences. If kids want to have fun, they have to create it themselves. The business or lemonade stand kids develop can be as wild and fun as their imaginations allow.

Kids should be able to take ideas from this book and apply them to business. The more ideas they have to work with, the greater the challenge and fun. We want younger kids to consider the fun of developing and possibly running a lemonade stand and older kids to think about all the potential opportunities that could arise in developing and running their own businesses.

Fun activities:

- A drawing exercise, where kids can draw a lemonade stand and advertising signs
- A writing exercise as kids write out a plan for their lemonade stands or business ideas
- A story telling exercise as kids tell others about their business stories
- A contest to engage kids to compete in business
- The basis for a teamwork initiative, which includes the school community and business partnerships

Developing Your Imagination - Putting Your Imagination To Work

"Imagination is more important than knowledge."
Albert Einstein.

Imagination is a creation of the mind and can lead to great ideas, which produces new inventions, improved products and changes the lives of many people.

Unfortunately, we don't take imagination or creative thinking courses in school, but these creative aspects are very important to idea generation. You will find the skill of imagination will evolve as you learn to ask questions and give plenty of thought to your answers.

There are progressive companies such as 3M who encourage their employees to use their imaginations and think about new ideas. This approach has lead to the development of many new products and greater business success. We would like you to use this book to further develop your thinking skills.

Everyone knows kids have great imaginations and we encourage kids to use their imaginations as they explore business. Throughout this business guide, kids will be asked questions which will put their imaginations to work, helping them create ideas for their businesses.

The combination of imagination and reality is also a good experience. It is a good idea to see how your business plan performs in a real business.

It is fun to imagine the ultimate lemonade stand or your great business idea!

Home Schooling And Tutoring

This book is a good resource for people who practice home schooling full time or on a supplemental tutoring basis. We encourage adults to participate in this experience with kids. This approach helps kids understand business and helps adults to convey important guidance and experiences.

The tutoring industry has grown dramatically in recent years, as parents are concerned for their child's preparation into university, college and a career. We believe that kids can enhance their school education with the right programming and support at home.

A little planned quality time a home with parental support is a very effective tutoring program. This is a great opportunity to interact with kids about business in the supportive environment of a home. A few "business meetings at home" would be a very interesting and great learning experience.

Kid's Business Club

This business guide is a great opportunity to put a "business club" together to explore business with friends. Organize a group of kids and sit down together to figure out how the group can attack the ideas in this book. Try the idea of a "DAB Club" or a "Kid's Business Club."

Competition or Contest

This book provides opportunities to create a friendly competition in developing a business. For many kids who need competition to spark their interest, we have listed some ideas:

Compete for different categories (design, advertising, product taste)
Run a school lemonade stand convention or business convention with a panel of judges awarding prizes
Have the local media do reporting and judging during a period of time
Ask a youth service group to sponsor a contest or competition on plans for lemonade stands and actual operating stands
Make a submission to the www.teachingkidsbusiness.com/lemonade-stand-awards.htm

Developing Commercial Opportunities For Kids

This book will help kids and adults consider commercial opportunities for kids. The thought of developing a business and learning to create a business will lead to other opportunities.

This book gives interesting opportunities for kids to consult other kids on developing a lemonade stand business. Kids would hire other kids to assist in the set-up and running of their lemonade stand business. They could be "lemonade stand consultants".

Our DAB applies to many other business opportunities, which kids could develop.

Check out www.teachingkidsbusiness.com - Kids-Works-Ventures.

Check out www.kidse-marketplace.com for other business opportunities for kids.

Chapter 4

Introduction To Develop A Business – DAB

In This Chapter

The Business Case Of Little Johnny And The Lemonade Stand
DAB – Develop A Business – Explained
How DAB Can Help You Succeed In Business
Let's Start To Develop A Business
The Fun Side Of Business
Developing Your Product or Service
Naming Your Product – Creating A Brand
Naming Your Business

The Business Case Of Little Johnny And The Lemonade Stand

Let's take an example of one approach in developing a business and use the classic example of the lemonade stand. We will use a fictional character called little Johnny who can represent any kid. Girls can imagine Little Mary as the character. Little Johnny has decided to set-up a lemonade stand business.

Little Johnny decided to set-up a lemonade stand on Saturday morning. He asked his mother to make some lemonade while he set-up a chair and a table by the end of his driveway. Little Johnny was up and running his lemonade stand business in less then an hour, but by business standards Little Johnny was not organized to do business. He wasn't sure what pricing to use, if people would like the taste of his lemonade and he had only told his Mom about opening his stand. Little Johnny had an enjoyable day talking to the few neighbours who passed his stand and felt he was successful selling a few glasses of lemonade.

If little Johnny was given some good advice such as how to DAB (develop a business), he could have taken some time to plan his business. Then he would have been busy serving people, rather than waiting for customers. Little Johnny still had a business experience but he could have got a lot more out of it.

If you are like little Johnny and just want to get started in business quickly, then you will benefit the most from this book. There are times when you have to move quickly and take advantage of opportunities in business. We are not suggesting that you will not succeed if you charge into an opportunity without some planning, but if you can master the business planning process, then you will have a better chance of succeeding.

We have learned from business experiences like little Johnny's and they have helped us develop our DAB approach. Throughout this book we will refer to the lemonade stand business to explain and demonstrate our DAB approach in planning a business.

Please keep in mind that little Johnny's business experience can be learned from and applied to many other businesses you may be considering.

DAB - Develop A Business - Explained

This is where you start to play around with business as you develop a business. Please remember that you are in charge of the amount of fun you have while learning about and developing a business. If you missed "The Fun Side Of Business" in Chapter One, you may want to take a moment and review it.

DAB means to "develop a business", any kind of business. Our DAB approach uses terms that are commonly used in business. We **define** the business term (like a dictionary does), we discuss the term to explain how it is used in the business world and we **apply it to a lemonade stand business**. DAB is really just helping you think about business. If you go through our DAB planning activity, you will be able to develop many different businesses from it.

23

As you go through our DAB section, please keep in mind many of the little steps that are taken to develop a business exist as real careers (jobs) for people. Decisions in business are made by people with the job of applying their skills and talents to help the business succeed. You will be exposed to various responsibilities and gain some experience as you take on the responsibility of various jobs. This experience will hopefully help you recognize what interests you in business, identify your talents, specific skills you have and skills you could work on.

As you develop a business you will try and do many different jobs by yourself, but soon realize you will need help. You will need a team of people who have different skills and talents to help you plan and succeed in business. You will probably have more fun working with a team, as you can bounce ideas off one another.

The decisions and the way you manage your business will determine how successful you are. You will need to constantly review your plan to ensure you are doing a good job and staying on track. The DAB approach should be reviewed and updated as your business develops.

The DAB section gives a very detailed framework of things to think about while developing a business. There are lots of steps to take and lots of questions to help you think through the development of your business. Use as much or as little information as you want.

How DAB Can Help You Succeed In Business

" The secret to success is to do the common things uncommonly well."
John D. Rockefeller Jr.

This phrase applies to what we are doing in this book. We show kids "common things" (steps or business decisions) that must be considered to develop a business. The success you have will come from how creative you are and how "uncommonly well" you apply the steps in business.
"The will to win is useless without the will to prepare."
Henry David Thoreau

As you go through our DAB section, you will learn how to prepare and plan a business. This process is where your imagination is put to work by coming up with great business ideas that will help you develop a business.

Our DAB approach asks you questions rather then giving you all the answers. We believe if you can learn to ask the right questions in business, you are more likely to come up with the answers. Most of us know how to use resources (books, Internet, people) to find answers, but if we don't know what answers to look for, we are not likely to get the answers we require.

Let's DAB by planning the development of a lemonade stand business or any business you choose. You have a lot of things to consider and decisions to make. You can make it as simple or sophisticated as you like. In any business, the more thought you put into planning (developing it right from the start), the higher the chances of your success. Please keep in mind you shouldn't think so much that you don't take action.

We have learned little Johnny could have been better prepared to go into business. We are happy to see a lot of kids trying out business ventures and getting their friends involved in it. We hope we can help kids who are considering business to make it a successful and fun experience.

Please don't judge the successes of your first few businesses by the amount of money you make or by how well people like your business ideas. The business experiences you have will prepare you for future success in business. At this stage in your business career, the focus should be on learning about and preparing for business. Take chances with innovative ideas.

"A smart businessperson is one who makes a mistake, learns from it, and never makes it again. A wise businessperson is one who finds a smart business person and learns from him how to avoid the mistakes he made."
Jim Abrams

Let's Start To Develop A Business

This is when you start using your imagination to DAB - asking and answering business questions, making business decisions and having some fun!

It is your choice on how you approach business:

- Read through this section to acquaint yourself with business
- Use it as a reference to further develop a number of business ideas you may have
- Go through this section to experience the planning and development of a lemonade stand business, which you may or may not choose to operate
- Use this section in a number of ways to help you think about business in ways you may not have considered before

To develop a business you will need to start somewhere. We would like you to have some fun with business so we are going to have you think about the "fun side" of your business. After you have figured out how to have some fun with your business, you can start developing a product and your business. We have used the next 7 sections to discuss things you should consider to help you develop a business. The sections are not in any particular order, but you can browse through the pages and focus first on the areas that interest you the most. The detailed table of contents will help you find areas of interest.

You will find as you complete one section you may think of something that applies to another section. Go back to any section at any time and reconsider it. To successfully develop any business, all the decisions you make have to work well together to reach the goals of the business. It is like a sports team that needs to work well together to win.

Your main goal should be to develop a business by considering and applying the DAB approach. Your business will have a greater chance of succeeding if you complete the whole DAB section.

We recommend that you take a pad of paper and create a heading (title) for each of the DAB topics that you work through. It is helpful to put the book's page number on the top of each of your written pages so that you can reference back to the book more easily. Use one page per DAB topic since you will likely add to each section as you go

through the process. You don't want to try and jam additional writing in between lines or have to draw arrows to the back of the page.

On each of the pages that you set-up for the topics in this book, try and answer the questions and make notes on your ideas. The answers and ideas that you come up with will be your plan to develop a business. Keep your pages in a binder or in a file folder where you can easily find them and make reference to them.

You can answer the questions to develop a lemonade stand business as a business experience or you can consider the questions and apply them to your own business idea. Work at your own pace and have a great business experience!

Have fun and enjoy your venture into business! Remember, business is really a game. Figure out how to play the game and you will succeed in business.

The Fun Side Of Your Business

If you are just interested in developing a business that makes money and having fun is not a very important factor, then you can ignore this section (jump to the next page) and use this guide to help you develop a business with the things that are important to you.

Now that you have decided you want to have some fun, this is your opportunity to have as much fun as you want with your business.

We all know what is fun and what is not fun. Most of us know when we need to be focussed and learn, and when to let loose and have fun. We are taught when we can have fun and we learn how to have fun. When we take a minute and think about business, we don't usually think about fun or play time.

The interesting challenge is how you can make this business experience fun when it may not appear to be fun from the start. Business may not appear to be fun, but fun can be created and found. Throughout this book we would like to challenge you to have fun, to create fun opportunities and help bring the "fun side" to your business experiences.

Apply to a lemonade stand business or a business of your choice

- Throughout this book we make references to a lemonade stand business, to help you better relate to the business topics. We would like you to reference "your idea of fun" as you explore business.
- Create the job of "Vice President of Fun" for your business. The person who holds this job is responsible for making sure your business experience involves some fun. If this becomes your responsibility, do the best job you can do at creating fun.
- Let the "Vice President of Fun" figure out how much fun your business needs, how to create more fun in your business experience, how fun contributes to the success of a business and how to balance fun with a successful business.
- Throughout this book think of the phrase, "How can I make this fun?" The amount of fun you think about is only limited by your imagination. The amount of fun you actually have with your business experience is your choice.
- How do you make your lemonade stand business fun?

Developing Your Product or Service

To be in business you need to offer a product or service. This is where your imagination can go wild. You can think of any product you want to create or start with making a lemonade drink product.

A product is anything that can be offered to a market (group of people) for attention, for purchase, to use, or to consume that might satisfy a need. Many products exist around you at home, at school, in shopping malls and grocery stores everywhere. Products range from toys, food, clothing, cars, games, etc.

For a product to be successful, you need people to want it or have a demand for it. It makes sense to understand the needs of people so that you can provide products they are interested in buying. It is also possible for innovative products to create new markets or needs for people.

In business, you want to understand what makes your product special, what are the benefits of your product, why customers are interested in your product and how it is different from other products.

You need to develop a product people want and you can produce with good quality, reliability and value. You need to figure out ways to make and sell the product such that you can recover your costs and make money (profit).

If you are offering a service, you want to offer a service people need and value. The key to service is to understand how to do it well and to provide it at a price that makes people feel you are offering good value (deal).

Apply to a lemonade stand or your business of choice

Developing a product using the example of lemonade:

- What kind of lemonade (product) will people like? (Taste)
- What should it look like? (Colour)
- What ingredients are important to people? (Real lemons, sugar as sweetener)
- Do some research and development. What is on the market and what do people like? Try developing products with different ingredients
- Write the steps out as if you were teaching someone how to make your product. In business this would be called a manual to train someone
- Are you going to buy an established brand of lemonade and sell it at your stand?
- Give some thought as to why products exist and use that thinking to develop your product
- Have you developed a secret formula for your lemonade?
- You may have created something that may be famous someday. Take the time to write out your formula and copyright it with "© 2003 (year), your first and last name"

Naming Your Product - Creating A Brand

You are certainly aware of the many brand names you buy. You buy some items because of the image the product has, rather than the usefulness it may or may not have.

A brand is a name, term, symbol, or design that is intended to clearly identify and differentiate a seller's product from the competitors' products. A brand name is used to identify a specific product.

The goal of any business is to have their brand recognized by, used by and referred to as many people as possible. Businesses spend a lot of time and money naming and developing their brand names.

The naming of your product can be a great experience and you should have lots of fun trying some wild names.

Apply to a lemonade stand or your business of choice

You will want to consider choosing a brand name for your lemonade to help people distinguish your product from others. Remember, your product is not just lemonade!

Give your product a brand name like "Tyler and Hayley's Tasty Real Lemonade."
The name you choose is your brand to allow people to remember your product by name rather then just by the taste of your lemonade.

Some things to consider when naming your product:

- Will my product name be remembered? When a name is different or unusual, it may attract attention and perhaps arouse curiosity
- Is it something that is interesting, such as a rhyme or humour? A good example is Toys-R-Us™ (Trademark owned by Toys-R-Us)
- Should my product name create a mental picture of an image? The Apple, provides an image that is easy to remember
- If the name is meaningful and fits with the product, it tends to generate higher recognition

- A two-syllable word will be easier to learn than a three-syllable word. For example, one-syllable words that are easily remembered are Coke™ and Bic™ (Trademarks owned by the respective companies)
- Will the name support a symbol or slogan? Example: Apple Bank – provides access to the associations of apples – something good, wholesome, and simple – it suggests a friendly, fun and somewhat different bank
- What do people think of the word? Is there a strong association with it? When Jell-O™ brought in the name Jigglers™, the name produced a strong visual image (Jell-O jiggling in the hand) and could be associated with jolly, happy people, good times and it's a kid's word (Trade mark is the property of Kraft)
- Is it distinct enough from other names, to prevent people from confusing your product with another?

Brand Extension (additional products)

Once you have developed your brand and succeeded in business with it, you may want to consider a brand extension. A brand extension is using a successful brand name to launch a new or modified product in a separate category. A successful brand helps businesses enter new product categories more easily. A frozen lemonade product would be a brand extension from your fresh lemonade drink product.

If you have established a name in your neighbourhood for washing cars, you will have an easier time launching a bicycle washing business.

Naming Your Business

This is a very challenging and fun exercise. If you have named a pet, you know what you need to think about and the choices you have. When you name your business you want to make sure other people like your business name and can remember it easily.

Every business needs a name. You can make it as simple as your net name, real name, your dog's name or create a name that makes sense with the type of business you are developing. This is an interesting experience to go through.

Once you have your product figured out, your business name is easier to develop. Therefore, you can come back to this section later if you still don't know what you are selling yet.

Be careful that your business name does not limit you to the products and services you can successfully offer. If you choose a name like "Sam's Sports Reviews" for your business name, you are going to restrict yourself to writing only sports reviews. People would not likely approach your business looking for travel reviews or information on travel.

The risk of tying your business name to your product is that you may have difficulty in the future when you want to launch different products. There have been situations where a clock shop wants to sell music. Would you think of going to Martha's Clock Shop to buy a CD?

Apply to a lemonade stand or your business of choice

- Create a list of business names you think will work
- Try some names that rhyme and think of some names that are funny
- Write the names out using different fonts and see how they look
- Think how your choice of names will work as a web site name
- Create a business naming contest for your family and friends to enter
- Think about cultural and language translation issues with various names (ie. Coca Cola has different meanings in Japan and North America)

Once you have chosen your business name, consider creating some business cards. Business cards are a helpful tool when you start promoting your business.

Chapter 5

Location, Design and Operation Of Your Business

In This Chapter

Location Of Your Business
Building/Facilities Design
Hours of Operation

Location Of Your Business

Where would you really like to work or operate your business? Dream a little and see how many great places you can come up with. Consider factors that are important to you and your business when you choose a location.

Location is where you choose to operate your business. Consider the country, city, area and then a specific address.

One of the most important decisions for any business is its location. You need to determine where to make the product, sell it and manage the business.

There are many considerations when choosing the location of your business. The best decisions balance the costs and benefits of the location, access to your customers, availability of workers, availability of products and services required in your business and other factors.

Apply to a lemonade stand or your business of choice

In the case of the lemonade stand business you are fortunate to have easy access to lemons or lemonade mix, water and ice. The people who will help at the stand will probably live nearby in your neighbourhood and your customers will also live close by.

Things to consider for your location selection:

- Where would a really great location be?
- Where is a good spot that is safe, but is visible to potential customers?
- Research a variety of locations, make notes and take pictures
- Can people stop their car, bike or walk safely to your location and approach the stand easily?
- Look at traffic, the flow of people at different locations. The more people that pass by a location, the better your chances of selling your product
- A friend's house may be a good location
- Do you and the people working with you (staff/associates) have access to washrooms?
- What happens if you run out of lemonade? Are you close to a location where more can be made or stored for back-up inventory?
- Are there restrictions on the location you are considering? Do you need a permit?
- Is there an area for your customers to enjoy their lemonade – chairs and tables like a café?
- Can you and your associates get there easily (commute time)?
- How does this location compare in cost (is there rent for the location)?
- How far is your location away from your competitors?
- Consider locating near a baseball park during a game or tournament
- Consider locating at garage sales
- Consider why your backyard may not be a great location

In business, people often say "location, location, location" because it is a very important element of business.

Building/Facilities Design

This is a great opportunity to think about your dream office and business building. How cool is your business going to look?

Business buildings or facilities are terms for the type of building or working space that is needed for a business.

Businesses need a place to do business. Most businesses will rent/lease space in traditional retail malls or commercial buildings. Many small businesses start out of a home, often in a basement or garage. As the business grows, the needs for space change and businesses will move.

Many businesses will alter the space they are renting to make it suit their type of business and the way they operate their business. Some businesses have the luxury of designing and building what they feel is the right facility for them. Businesses need to have appealing space to do what they do, to provide customers with an enjoyable experience and employees with a safe and productive work environment.

Apply to a lemonade stand or your business of choice

- What do you want your lemonade stand to look like? Make a rough sketch of it
- Consider the type of space you need (lemonade stand sales facility, warehousing and production)
- Consider hiring someone to design your stand
- Do you build it or buy it?
- How do you want customers to approach and use the stand and the area around it?
- What things can you do to make it comfortable for the workers?
- What things can you do to make the lemonade stand work well or to make it easier to serve and be served?
- What can you do to make your stand attract and satisfy customers? What are the costs of your ideas and can your business afford to pay for these ideas?
- Where will you produce the lemonade – what space will you need?
- Where will you store your supplies, your stand and your lemonade?
- What features are important to the people who work in your business, your customers and people that supply goods for your business?

Hours Of Operation

Hours of operation are the hours in a day and the days in which a business is open for business.

If you are not open for business you cannot do any business. The Internet is really an exception to normal business hours since you can do business 24/7/365. You can imagine how difficult it would be for a store or other kinds of businesses to be open 24/7/365.

All businesses have to decide when they will be open and closed for business. There are many factors that have to be considered when making this decision.

- When can you schedule your time to mange the business?
- When do your customers need your product or services?
- When are people available to work? Can you get people to work if you do not offer enough hours of work in a day, week or year?
- When is your competition open?
- Can you afford to open at times when there is not enough business to pay for the costs of being open?
- Are there restrictions where you are located? Does the building you operate in have any restrictions? Does the area have restrictions on running a business?

Apply to a lemonade stand or your business of choice

- When should you start your business? (Month)
- What days should you serve lemonade?
- How many hours a day should you operate?
- How many hours a day should be planned for preparation and after closing duties?

Chapter 6

Market For Your Product

In This Chapter

Market
Going Global
Competition

Market

The market for a product is the demand for a particular product or service. The market has to do with the size (number of people, dollar sales) and make up (age, male/female, culture) of the customers that could buy your product. The market size is usually measured by sales during a specified period of time, such as a million dollars per year.

A lot of businesses start selling to family, friends and local area but quickly realize they need more people to sell to. The ideal situation is to have a big market for your product. Businesses are constantly trying to increase their market share by making their products available to more customers, by making more customers aware of the product, by expanding the geographic areas where the product is available and by changing the product to increase the demand.

Before any business gets started, it is important to understand how big the market is for a product. If there is no market for the product or the market is not large enough to make money, then the business will not succeed.

Apply to a lemonade stand or your business of choice

- How many people will pass by your stand? Take a pad of paper and try to do a people count in your area. Check out the population data for your area
- How many people will know about your stand?
- How many people do you think will visit your business?

- What are the ages of the people who will buy your product?
- Try and describe who your customers are and how many you could possibly have
- If your product is very sour, you will limit the size of your market because people who like sweeter things will not buy your product. Is the market bigger for sweet or sour lemonade?
- How many dollars worth of lemonade do you think you will sell per day, per month, per year?

Going Global

Going global is marketing a product throughout the world with the same brand name. Going global or international is the dream of most businesses. When a company goes global, the number of people who may purchase their product around the world is increased substantially. This is very attractive to most companies because the market potential is huge, but there are many obstacles to deal with. There are issues of language, different cultural needs, logistics of getting products to or making products in other markets and the economics of doing business in other markets.

Apply to a lemonade stand or your business of choice

- Do you have a product that people in other countries would like to buy?
- Could your business go global by selling in other countries?
- What are some of the things you would have to consider before going global? (Translation of your product name and advertising)
- Think big. Which countries do you think are good opportunities for global expansion? Do some research on these countries

Competition

Most of us are competitive by nature. We want to win. We want to beat the other person at the game. Business is really the same as any game with competition. Competition is a rivalry or someone else trying to do the same or similar thing you are doing.

Competition in business is no different than sports. You are competing or doing business against other businesses or teams of people. Your competition is trying to win by selling more products than your business and getting your customers to buy their products.

In all types of businesses it is important to understand your competition. If you plan to go into business and provide a product that is already being supplied by someone else, then you will have to do it much better, give better value or offer it at a better price to take business away from your competition.

If you have an original business idea and you are the first to take it to market, you will still have to consider the threat of competition in the future.

Apply to a lemonade stand or your business of choice

- Is there competition in your area? Are there other kids or businesses selling lemonade or cold drinks where you are planning to do business?
- You need to act like an investigator and find out what is going on in your market
- What product is your competition selling?
- How is your competition selling their product?
- What are they selling their product for? (Price)
- How big are their servings? How good is their product?
- In what ways is your competition better? (ie. Is their product sweeter?) What are they doing better or differently than you?
- What things can you do to win over your competition? (Get their customers to your stand)
- What will you do if someone copies your idea and opens a stand across the street from you (or near by)?

Chapter 7

Marketing Your Product

In This Chapter

Marketing
Packaging
Pricing
Advertising
Promotion
Special Events
Word of Mouth
Publicity
Press Release
Reputation
Market Research
Focus Groups

Marketing

Marketing is concerned with attracting customers, raising awareness of your product, getting people to buy, making sure that customers are happy with their purchase so they come back for more.

Marketing impacts many different activities such as sales, advertising, customer service, the product development, pricing and discounts, reputation, distribution, promotions and much more. Marketers act as the product's parent, guiding many aspects of the product's life.

Marketing is the process of planning and executing the conception, pricing, promotion, and distribution of ideas, products, and services to create exchanges that will satisfy the needs of individuals and organizations.

Marketing focuses on identifying the customer's needs and preferences. Using this information, a company can shape the goods and services it provides and the strategy it uses to bring these goods and services to the public so that the customer is satisfied.

We will deal with many of the marketing elements throughout the DAB section.

Apply to a lemonade stand or your business of choice

- How are you going to make people want your product?
- How are you going to identify your customers' needs and preferences?
- How are you going to get the message out about your brand of lemonade?
- How are you going to tell people what is special about your product?
- How will you let people know where you are and what you are doing?
- How are you going to position (way you want people think of) your business?
- What steps are you going to take to make sure your product will be in demand by customers?

Packaging

Packaging is the design of wrappers or containers for a product. Packaging is also how the product is presented to customers.

Businesses put a lot of thought into the overall look of a product. The choice of colours, shape, graphics and text are all important business decisions.

Packaging is often an important consideration for customers since people are not likely to buy something that they do not like the look of.

We have all bought things because of the way they look; therefore you know good packaging can really sell products.

Apply to a lemonade stand or your business of choice

Take a paper and pencil and draw some packaging ideas. Use some cool graphics and colours. Look at some packaging ideas in stores and products at home to get some ideas.

Consider how your product looks as it is presented to your customers.
- Size of glass
- Colour of glass
- Consider packaging if you were to bottle your lemonade (label, container design)

Other considerations:

- Appearance of your stand
- It is important to figure out how your stand should look and what the overall experience at the stand should be
- Appearance of the people working at the stand (ie. Uniforms)
- Appearance of the area around the stand

Pricing

You know things appear to be to expensive when you are a kid with little money. Businesses would like to sell products at a really low price if they could still make lots of money.

Pricing is the amount of money charged for a product or service, or the value a consumer exchanges for the benefit of having a product or service. Pricing is how much a product is sold for.

Pricing is an important decision you need to make and one that has to be reviewed constantly. If your price is too high, people will not buy your product. If it is too low, you may not be recovering your costs and therefore will not make a profit. If people can buy a similar product for less from a competitor nearby, then they will probably go to your competitor unless you have created a reason for them to prefer your brand.

You also have to consider the impact the price will have on the number of products you sell. If you lower your price by 10% and sell 30% more product, you made a good decision. This concept is called contribution. You may contribute more money to cover your costs if you sell more products at a lower cost or more products in general.

It is important to understand how much it costs to make and sell your product. Once you know your costs, you can figure out the selling price of your product to make different profit levels. This only works if your customers are willing to pay your price.

It is important to understand what price your customers are willing to pay for your product. You can ask customers what they think is a fair price and adjust your price as you operate your business. You can also justify a higher price by providing good value (additional quality, services, etc.).

Apply to a lemonade stand or your business of choice

- How much are you going to sell your lemonade for? What is the price of a bottle or can of lemonade in stores? What is the price at other lemonade stands?
- How much does it cost you to make your lemonade?
- How much does it cost you to sell your lemonade?
- Will you change your price based on sales levels?
- What does the price do to your sales?
- What does the price do to your profit?
- You should also look at adjusting your serving sizes. This is another way of changing your pricing. If you sell a smaller serving and hold your price, then you are increasing your price.
- What can you do to provide better value for the price you set?

Advertising

All kids are experts on what is good and bad advertising. Have some fun thinking and creating your own advertisements. You can write it, draw or go wild and film your own commercials.

Advertising is a communications that is paid for by an identified sponsor with the goal of building awareness of a particular brand, product or service over a long period of time.

In order to create awareness for your product, you want to break through all the clutter of advertising in your market by clearly communicating the name of your brand; its key features and benefits in a way that will make people want to buy your product. You want to communicate a brand message to a large audience.

Great advertising can be very powerful. It can make you feel something about a brand – happy or sad. Advertising typically communicates a message to a large audience through print or television, attempting to provide viewers with a better understanding of what a brand is all about.

Apply to a lemonade stand or your business of choice

You have seen lots of advertising on TV, on road signs, in magazines, on web sites and e-mails. You know what attracts your eye and what it takes to get you to buy a product. You need to figure out the same for the people you are selling to.

- What is the best way to convey your lemonade brand ideas in a cool way while getting people to purchase your product?
- What message will you need to create to get people to buy your product and to insure they want to buy your lemonade?
- Will "Lemonade For Sale" be good enough advertising?
- What can you do that is better and different to spark some interest?
- Try and write a radio advertisement for your business
- Create a "jingle" which is a little song about your product – catchy and memorable that people will enjoy and remember

- Check out the classified listing in your paper or community bulletin boards as a way to post the information about your business. You may want to run a classified ad or post on a community bulletin board
- Local businesses (grocery stores) may allow you to post a notice on their notice board of your upcoming lemonade stand
- What other ways can you advertise your business?
- Have some fun creating an advertisement or act out a commercial in front of an audience (friends and family)

Promotion

You have seen lots of promotions targeted at kids. You know what works for you and your friends. Have some fun creating a great promotion with gifts and prizes that really rock.

Promotion is creating awareness and driving sales of a product. Promotions communicate the brand benefits at the point of purchase while providing some incentive for consumers to buy. These incentives may include a chance to win something by mailing in proof that you have bought the product or it may offer a "gift" with the purchase.

Unlike advertising, promotions tend to get people to react "now" to make a purchase. Usually promotions have a catchy phrase and some kind of prize or incentive to buy a product. Promotions encourage you to try or buy more of a product by offering value add (reason or additional value) in a way that is relevant to you (the target market).

You see promotions all the time. It might be a toy in a cereal box or a chance to win something if you fill out a contest form. The idea is to reward and encourage you to buy a product.

Apply to a lemonade stand or your business of choice

- What are you going to do to get people to try your product?
- How are you going to create some excitement about your lemonade stand?
- Maybe you want to run a promotion with a prize. The prize could be something you purchase or from another business that wants to use your business to promote theirs. What kind of prizes would your customers like?

- Create coupons (discount or free product) like the ones that come on cereal boxes, with a pizza delivery or in the mail. Figure out a way to get them into the hands of your potential customers
- What kind of coupons would work for your customers?
- Think of great promotions you have seen and try to adapt them to your business

Special Events

Imagine creating a really cool special event or locating your business where lots of people can participate in or watch great activities.

A special event is an activity that allows you to better understand a brand because you have the opportunity to actually "experience" it through an event. An event attracts people and holds their attention because a whole host of things happens at an event.

Once you attract people's attention, you have the opportunity to communicate and persuade your customers to purchase your product. For example, you may have been to a sporting event where you saw lots of product displays and advertisements. The combination of a great experience at an event and exposure to a product will influence you to buy a product.

Apply to a lemonade stand or your business of choice

This is a great opportunity to explore and demonstrate the "fun side of your business". Consider creating a fun event to attract people to your stand and show them how much fun and exciting your product and business is.

- Are you going to create a petting zoo with a friendly animal to bring additional excitement to your lemonade stand?
- What other events can you do to drive people to your stand?
- Do some research on events in your area and try and use some of these ideas in your business
- Consider garage sales as event opportunities

Word Of Mouth

Most of us have something to say about the latest movie, CD, toy etc. Think of the things you say and the things you hear from other people. Some businesses actually pay people to start saying good things about their products!

Word of mouth is the process in which the purchaser of a product or service tells friends, family, neighbours and associates about its benefits or what they like about the product or service.

The movie industry relies on word of mouth to spread the word about a good movie. It can be very powerful, particularly when it comes to passing information via the Internet. Think how quickly news of a good movie spreads among your friends.

Word of mouth is a great source of information for your product. People will often buy a product after hearing good things from a friend, family member or co-worker. You can't control what people say about your product, but you can influence word of mouth.

Apply to a lemonade stand or your business of choice

- Start telling people about your plans and encourage them to spread the word
- Make your product special in some way
- Give people something special to talk about
- Make the name of your product or business noteworthy/catchy
- Do something cool at your stand and associate it with your product
- Find people who you know will talk to other people and have them test your product and learn about what your business is doing
- Try some viral e-mail, otherwise known as e-mail word of mouth
- Think of things that you have said to other people about a product such as a movie, toy, game etc.
- Explore opportunities for a blog

Try a little word of mouth game:

Write down what you would like people to say about your lemonade stand business. Get a group of people together and sit in a circle. Whisper what you have written into the ear of the person next to you and have them do the same to the person next to them. Have the last person in the circle say out loud what they have been told. This will show you what might happen as your message is passed on from one person to another.

Reputation

We all have some kind of reputation. Smart, funny, a little crazy, etc. As you venture into business you start to think more about what people will think about you and your business. You want to have a good reputation so customers will keep coming back and you can attract new customers.

Reputation is the estimation in which a person or thing is commonly held, whether favourable or not. Reputation is character in the view of the public, the community, etc. Reputation is what people think of you.

Businesses work hard to develop and maintain a good reputation. The reputation of the people that operate the business is as important as is the way the business treats its customers, employees and suppliers.

If a business does not stand behind the product and services it provides, these actions will create a poor reputation. It takes hard work and a long time to create a good reputation, but only a short time to destroy it.

Apply to a lemonade stand or your business of choice

- Be aware that you have to treat people well. This includes the people who work for you, potential customers, customers and suppliers
- Keep in mind that your actions will determine what people think of you and what they will say about you and your business. Your actions determine your reputation and your success

- It is important to try and create the reputation of a hard-working, honest, good and enjoyable businessperson. What can you do to create a good reputation?
- Think of what you would like people to say about you and your business and try and take the right actions to develop a good reputation
- Who do you know has a good reputation and what kinds of things do they do?

Publicity

This is a hard thing for every business to do, but as a kid in business you may be able to get a little more attention then most businesses. Don't be afraid to say, "Hey I'm a kid - give me a break".

Publicity is coverage of your product or business in a news medium such as a newspaper, radio or TV.

Public relations (PR) are the active pursuit of publicity for marketing purposes. As a marketer you try and create good publicity. If you can create good stories and communicate them to the media effectively, there is a chance they will pick-up the stories and give you publicity.

If you are successful in getting good publicity, it will noticeably help your business. Once people are aware of your business, your chance of converting them to customers is greatly improved.

Press Release

An effective and quick format for communicating a story is a press release. A press release is a short written document with a clear headline at the top, followed by sufficient facts and quotes to support a short news story, brief background on the company/product, a date and contact information for journalists who want more information or an interview.

See chapter 12 - Press Release – for an example of a press release.

Basically you want to get your message out to the media and hope they will put it in the newspaper or magazine, etc.

Media businesses (newspapers, TV, etc.) receive many press releases each day. The media has to sort through them and decide which ones to follow up on based on what they think their audience will be interested in. The key is to try and find out how you can appeal to the media and its audiences.

Apply to a lemonade stand or your business of choice

Look at your local news coverage and try to identify the reporters or journalists you think might cover your story.

- Try and catch the attention of your local media (ie. Do a special event)
- How do you create awareness in your local newspapers or TV stations? Try and create a news story
- Prepare a press release to send out to newspapers and TV stations. Think of a clear message that answers the questions of who, what, where, when, why and "how". Find an angle that creates some interest for the media to cover your story.

Basically you want to create an approach that attracts media attention and one that will interest your local customers.

Market Research

Businesses spend a lot of money trying to figure out what is important to kids and why they purchase things. You have a great advantage in this area because you know what kids like.

Market research is the use of data (information) to resolve concerns businesses have about their marketing.

This is a helpful business approach taken by companies who want to gain greater confidence in what they are planning to do. It is better to use this approach to learn what people think about your product and the way you market to them, before you start selling on a large scale.

Apply to a lemonade stand or your business of choice

- Think of questions you would like answered and find the answers
- The cheapest and most effective way for you to obtain answers will probably be to ask people or conduct your own market research
- There are businesses you can buy answers and theories from
- There are articles, books and web sites that may have some of the answers
- What do consumers want?
- Do you know the behaviour of your customers?
- Who will buy it?
- How do they like it?
- When will they buy it?
- How much will they pay?
- What size of servings do they like?
- What type of packaging do they like?
- Research lemonade that is sold by big companies and see what they are doing
- Can you think of other questions you would like answered?

Focus Groups

A focus group is a bunch of people who are brought together for the purpose of getting their opinions on a particular product or concept. Focus groups are used to test products and concepts before they are sold in the marketplace.

A lot can be learned from focus groups. People's opinions on a product or service can often lead to changes that will help the product be better received in the marketplace. It is a neat experience to sit down with a group of people and discuss what they did or did not like about a product.

Apply to a lemonade stand or your business of choice

Consider organizing a focus group to help you test your product and your business approach. This will help you to ensure that people will like your product before you go selling it and they like the way you are going to do business.

There are lots of questions you must find the answers to:

- Do people like your product?
- Do people like the taste?
- Do they like the look of your product?
- Do they like the serving size?
- Do they like the price?
- Do they like the physical appearance of your lemonade stand?
- Do they like the way you serve it?
- Get responses on ideas you have for promotions and advertisements
- Think of other questions. Look at questions you developed in your market research section
- Test your ideas for fun in your business
- Test your ideas for special events
- Test your ideas on your location choice

Here is a new activity for a party. Try sitting together and brainstorm on a business idea, new product or get some feedback on a business idea you have.

Chapter 8

Operations And Administration Of Your Business

In This Chapter

Customer Service
Distribution
Supplies
Quality Control
Safety
Security
Technology Management
Information Technology (IT)

Customer Service

Customer service is how you treat your customers before, during and after a sale. It is the services a business offers to its customers, especially when buying consumer goods such as a computer and car. Customer service includes the initial buying, questions about a product, repair and replacement service, extended guarantees, regular communications of information, telephone and e-mail follow-up and complaint handling.

The level of customer service greatly affects how customers think about a company. Companies thrive to provide a service level that stands out and exceeds a customer's expectations. The companies that succeed with customer service understand what they are doing and are always looking for ways of exceeding a customer's expectations.

All businesses have to understand how to serve customers. Any time a customer or potential customer contacts a business, good customer service should be practiced. Obviously the better you treat a customer, the happier they will be and the more likely they will purchase from you in the future.

It is one thing when a business provides excellent customer service, but the reality is, there is a cost to customer service and sometimes businesses can't afford the ideal level of customer service. There is also a cost to the business for bad customer service and that cost is lost sales from losing customers.

Most people have had a bad customer service situation in which they were not handled fairly and walked away disappointed. Many of these people probably did not do business again with that company and went to buy from the competition. In fact, for every one person that complains about bad service, there are many more who don't complain but will never do business with that company again!

The main goal of customer service should be to respond to a customer in a way that leaves a lasting positive impression. When you examine customer service, think of the little things that are important to people and how a company can address these areas.

Apply to a lemonade stand or your business of choice

This is an excellent opportunity for you to understand how to succeed at customer service. If you can understand and manage this important business principle, you are well on your way to success.

- How can you make your lemonade stand a great experience for customers?
- What do you think are important customer service elements? Consider a clean stand, music, friendly service, smiling and welcoming staff, car & bicycle washing services and newspapers or magazines at the stand while they enjoy their drink
- Think of excellent customer service experiences you have had in other businesses - try and adapt them to your business
- Develop a checklist of things you will do in your business to provide excellent customer service
- Try this little game. Act out some of the worst service experiences you have had or could possibly have. Laugh and learn from this

Distribution

Distribution of your product is to do with the ways in which you get your produce out to your customers.

Once you have developed a product, you will proceed to produce a quantity for your customers. Distribution is the process of moving the product from where it is produced to where customers can buy it. Every business has to figure out the best way to do this, given the resources and money they have to spend.

There are businesses that distribute products for manufacturers. The manufacturer of the product sends the product right from the factory to the distributor. The distributor receives the product and then sells it to businesses that will sell it to the consumers. Distributors make sense if they do a good job of selling your product and can do it cheaper then you could do yourself.

Apply to a lemonade stand or your business of choice

- Have you considered ways to get your products in the hands of customers?
- Could you package and sell your product to other lemonade stands or to stores?
- If you were to choose stores to sell your product, which stores would you choose? Why would they want your product instead of another product?
- Could you take orders and have it delivered when and where your customer wants it?
- Could you distribute a manufacturers product to other businesses?

Supplies

Supplies are the items needed in business to help people get their jobs done. Supplies include paper, pens, business cards, file folders etc. Supplies help you do jobs such as organize your business, make presentations, clean and operate your business.

You know what it is like to purchase all the neat things you need for school - paper, pens, pencils, binders and rulers. There are many more supplies used by employees to do their jobs.

Apply to a lemonade stand or your business of choice

You will need lots of items to get your business ready for operation. Have some fun planning what you would like to have, determine what you really need and then figure out what you can afford to buy.

Lemonade Stand Supplies
- Paper for signs and posters
- Markers for designing and colouring your advertising
- Table and chairs
- Cash box

Lemonade Supplies

- Water
- Glasses
- Ice
- Lemonade ingredients, (lemons, sugar or lemonade powder)
- Containers to hold the lemonade

Operation of the Lemonade Stand Supplies

- Cleaning supplies
- Pen and a pad of paper to plan your stand
- Note pad for ideas on how to develop and improve your business
- Paper for accounting to keep track of all your sales, expenses and staffing schedules
- File folders to organize your business documents
- Check out an office supply catalogue or go to an office supply store to get ideas for things you may need for your business

Quality Control

Quality control is about developing rules, tests and ensuring you take the right steps to provide a good reliable product that people can rely on to be good each and every time they buy.

Quality control is the activities and techniques used to achieve and maintain a high standard of quality in a process. This procedure is concerned with finding and eliminating the causes of quality problems.

All businesses should be very aware of the quality control measures they have in place. You have probably heard company advertisements talk about how good and reliable their products are. You can imagine what would happen to a company that sold a product and it didn't work. People would return the product and the company would be out of business very quickly, since no one would buy from a company that makes lousy products.

There are many quality control systems available for businesses to ensure they take the steps to test the parts and overall product.

Apply to a lemonade stand or your business of choice

- What procedures are you taking to ensure a consistent taste, clean handling of your product and ingredients?
- Are the glasses clean, without cracks or chips?
- Is your stand clean and tidy?
- Make sure your employees wash their hands before and during work
- Do you have a quality checklist?
- Do you have a training system for employees?
- Research quality control systems (TQM – Total Quality Management, ISO and Six Sigma)

Safety

This is to do with freedom from danger, injury or damage, while you are at work. Safety relates to the employees, customers and suppliers who visit a business. It is important for any business to understand the risks and take steps to minimize the possibility of people getting hurt. This includes a broad range of factors from lifting things, operation and danger around machines, hazardous materials, traveling concerns, kidnapping etc.

Apply to a lemonade stand or your business of choice

- If you are using knives to cut lemons or a blender, make sure you take proper safety precautions - manuals often provide safety guidelines
- Think of things you can do to ensure safety in your business
- Please ensure you have discussed with an adult, your own safety and the safety of the people who are helping you at the stand
- Research employee safety standards with your government (web site)
- Research accidents that happened to people at work and learn from them

Security

Security is something that gives or assures safety. Security is taking steps to provide safety.
Businesses have to take a number of steps to ensure they have adequate security:

- Security guards will keep unauthorized people out of the workplace, prevent employees from walking out with company property and coordinate emergency operations – ambulance and fire
- Things are locked to prevent theft
- Computer access and access to certain areas is restricted to certain people
- Alarm systems are used to deter theft
- Some companies use video surveillance to monitor areas of the business
- Some people have security guards that travel with them

Apply to a lemonade stand or your business of choice

Make sure you consider ways to protect yourself, your employees, customers, product and items at your stand from being stolen or damaged by someone. Unfortunately, it is not always safe to be unattended at the side of any street.

- List a number of ways your business could use security
- You may want to operate your lemonade stand during a yard sale when adults can be working near by
- Pretend you are an uncover police officer and think of security weakness that your business has. What opportunities exist for potential crimes? How can you prevent them from happening?

Technology Management

Kids have grown up with technology and therefore adapt to the use and changes in technology very easily. As you develop a business you will naturally use technology to your advantage. This is a very interesting part of developing a business and one that you should spend time reviewing the many choices of technology.

Technology management is managing the use of technology in a business. (ie. Computers, fax machines, photocopiers, manufacturing equipment, phones, security systems, etc.)

Technology management has been one of the most important elements in business. Good technology management practices have made companies more competitive and more efficient. The proper use of technology will make businesses more profitable.

Apply to a lemonade stand or your business of choice

Technology use in your business can happen in many ways:

- Telephone or e-mail can be used to contact staff, customers, suppliers etc.
- Kitchen appliances can be used to make lemonade

- Web site development tools can be used to market your business on the Internet
- Computers can be used to plan and control your business

There are a number of steps for you to manage technology in your business - evaluation, selection, development, purchasing, implementation and disposal.

Examine these steps to determine how technology can be used in your business:

- Do some technology research and make a list of the technology that can be used in your business
- Think through the process of purchasing technology
- Evaluate - what do you need and what functions should the technologies have? (ie. Music player – radio, CD or DVD)
- Selection - what choice would you make from the available options - consider price and operating costs?
- Development - do you develop it or buy it? (Usually applies to computer software)
- Purchasing - think of how to negotiate the purchase of the technology and how to process the required information to buy it
- Implementation - think through how you will make the technology work in your business (Installing, training, maintaining, etc.)

Information Technology (IT)

Information technology is the use of computers and other electronic devices to process and distribute information. Given the exciting IT available to us today, this is an interesting and changing topic.

IT is an important part of business. Businesses know that computers and other information technologies are essential to help make the business run better. Computers make it easier to process and retrieve information. The use of information allows businesses to make decisions with timely and accurate information.

The IT industry changes very rapidly and there are new technologies on the market constantly. Businesses must assess the technologies and determine the costs and benefits of using these technologies.

Apply to a lemonade stand or your business of choice

Have some fun identifying all the technology you can use to make your business high-tech, fun and effective. Even dream of some technology that may not exist - you may be on to an invention and a new business opportunity.

There is a role for computers and other electronic devices (hand held devices, cell phones) in every business, including a lemonade stand.
A computer can be used to:

- Process information on sales of your product and other activities of your business
- Create your staffing plan
- Process your accounting information
- Create your advertising and promotional materials
- E-mail customers or potential customers to promote your business
- Develop and maintain a web site for your business
- Accept payment by e-mail (PayPal)

Other technologies can be used to exchange information and make your operations more efficient:

- A hand held device can be used for scheduling staff and keeping track of the things you have to do (To Do List), information about your customers and how they like their lemonade
- Two-way radios can be used between the stand, your home or with a partner
- A cell phone can be used for communications

Chapter 9

Managing People

In This Chapter

Staff Scheduling
Supervision
Motivating People
Human Resource Management (HRM)

You have been managed for years by your parents and teachers. You can probably recall many good ways and some not so good ways that you and others have been managed. Take these examples, learn from them and think about the way you would like to manage your business and the people involved in your business. Develop your own management style.

Staff Scheduling

A staffing schedule is a listing of who will do what jobs and when.
Businesses have to figure out how many people they need to run the business and when to use these employees. Basically, you want to be able to look at a calendar and show when people will work and what job they will be doing.
Businesses assign or delegate this responsibility to a manager or supervisor to ensure the schedule is made up and managed properly.

Apply to a lemonade stand or your business of choice

As you act as a manager and plan the scheduling of people, you will discover:
- Who makes decisions on pricing, serving sizes, advertising and the many other things to consider throughout this book
- Who, how and when will your stand be staffed?
- Who makes the lemonade?
- Who sets up the stand?

- Who sells it?
- Who puts the stand away?
- Identify other jobs and determine who will do them (getting ice, clean up)

Put a staffing schedule together (Example of headings below):

Date	Person Working	Job Responsibility	Time in (starting)	Time out (finished)
August 16	Mom	Making lemonade	10:00	10:45
August 16	Johnny	Serving	11:00	3:00
August 16	Mary	Serving	12:00	3:00
August 16	Dad	Clean-up	3:00	3:30

Supervision

Every kid has been supervised and knows how it works. Supervision is to oversee, direct or manage.

Supervision is normally provided by someone who has experience, is responsible and who can help people do their jobs and learn more skills.

Businesses have the need for supervision in a similar way that schools do. Teachers are supervisors who help keep control in the classroom and help kids get their work done. People working in business need supervision to make sure they are doing their jobs properly.

Supervisors also play important roles in training, scheduling of people, encouragement, performance feedback, communicating priorities and assigning the work that has to be done.

Apply to a lemonade stand or your business of choice

- This is an opportunity to develop as a supervisor. You can develop a plan for supervision and learn to supervise.
- Make sure your business has the right supervision

- What level of supervision do you think you need in your business? What level of supervision do your employees need?
- What makes a good supervisor?
- There may still be a role for some adult supervision!
- If you are cutting real lemons, have an adult cut them or train you how to do it. We don't want you to cut your fingers!
- Have an adult review and supervise your safety rules for your stand
- Discuss your overall DAB plan with an adult and ask for their advice and supervision

Motivating People

Motivating people is making sure people are keen or excited to do their work.

You have experienced a variety of motivating techniques that teachers use to motivate kids to pay attention and get their work done. You may not realize it, but at an early age you learned ways to motivate people. (ie. When you were a baby you learned to motivate your parents to feed you when you were hungry)

Learning how to motivate people is an important component of managing employees and running a business. People are motivated by money, personal development, their job and the way they are treated, among many factors. Since people are different and many jobs are different, it is important to understand the needs of the people you are trying to motivate. Whatever motivates you may not motivate another person who does the same job.

You will need to consider many things when you are structuring jobs. You want to consider and understand what is important to people and make sure you are doing the right things to motivate them so they do their jobs well.

Things to consider:

- Skill variety – the degree to which the job includes different activities involving several skills and abilities (People want a challenge)
- Task identity – the extent to which a person is able to complete a task from start to finish (People want to see results from what they have done)

- Task significance – the degree to which a person carrying out a task perceives it to be important to the organization and its clients (People want to feel that their job is important)
- Autonomy – the degree to which a person has the decision as to how and when the task will be done (People want to be empowered to make some decisions on how they do their job)
- Feedback – the extent to which the person receives feedback on the quality of performance from the task itself (People want to be told when they are doing a good job and how to improve)
- Rewarding people – how people are rewarded for their good work (acknowledgement, bonuses, trophies etc.)

Apply to a lemonade stand or your business of choice:

- Skills – identify the skills required to perform the various jobs involved in a lemonade stand business. Start with a listing of jobs and then write the skills required beside each job
- Task identity – come up with a way to determine how well a person completes a task (i.e. Pouring lemonade without spilling and pouring the right serving size)
- Task significance – find out from your employees how they think they are contributing to the business. Do they feel they are helping the business succeed?
- Autonomy – write out how employees can decide things on their own
- Feedback – develop an approach for telling your employees how they are performing

Human Resource Management (HRM)

Human resource management is a function in business that has become very interesting and very important. Businesses are starting to realize how important their employees (workers, staff) are. HRM deals with the "people part" of the business and ensures that the business has the right people for the job and treats them well.

HRM is the overall management of people in a business. It is the management of people to achieve individual behaviour and performance that will enhance an organization's effectiveness. HRM encourages individuals to set personal goals and creates rewards to shape their behaviour in accordance with the objectives of the organization. Get people to do a good job and reward them for it.

HRM deals with the:

- Morale of employees and the ways of achieving consistent job satisfaction
- Methods to select employees (Hiring)
- Setting of salaries (Pay)
- Training of employees
- Firing and outplacement of employees
- Performance setting and review of employees
- Benefits
- Policies and procedures (rules)
- Office hours
- Office space and furniture
- Company events and team building activities

Apply to a lemonade stand or your business of choice

If your business involves more than one person, there is a need for human resource management. Your business has a better chance of succeeding if the people working for you are happy, well trained and well suited for their jobs.

- Think of ways to motivate people to do a good job.
- List the employees you need - the type of employees needed to run the lemonade stand by position and required skills
- Determine an approach to find, interview and hire the necessary people - create a job advertisement, write out interview questions you would ask candidates, and draft an offer of employment to confirm the job offer
- Come up with a training process for new staff. What does new staff need to learn?
- Set the salary ranges (Pay) for various jobs
- Come up with incentive programs to encourage the staff to perform (bonus, toys, free product, paid days off or discounted products etc.)

Chapter 10

Money Side Of Your Business

In This Chapter

Financing A Business
Budgeting
Money Management
Payment Terms
Accounting
Advanced Accounting

Financing A Business

There are many good product and business ideas that never get started because of the difficulties in getting proper financing. Many businesses get started, but fail because of a lack of financing. Financing is an area that all business operators need to spend time on and understand.

Finance relates to the money aspects of your business, the practice of getting and managing money. Finance includes the capital involved in a project, especially the capital that has to be raised to start a new business.

Businesses need money to get started. You realize there are many steps to take to develop a business. Each of these steps requires money the business may not have. A business needs financing when it doesn't have the money it requires in the bank or is not taking in enough money to buy the things it requires.

Money is obtained from a person, bank, company or an investor. This money can be in the form of borrowing or capital. Borrowing means you use other people's money with the intent of paying it back, while you pay interest (regular payments) for the use of the money. Capital means the difference between assets and liabilities and is an amount that is not owed or borrowed.

Apply to a lemonade stand or your business of choice

Do an Internet search on "venture capital" and explore the process of financing a business. Examine the web sites of banks and governments to see available financing programs.

- How much money do you need? Once you have your budget (estimated costs) prepared you will need to raise (get) the money
- How will you get the money you need to start your business? You will require money (start-up capital) to buy the supplies and other things to get started.
- Play the role of a financier (person who gets financing), prepare a pitch (one page summary) and talk to people about putting money into your business venture. Answer the questions of - What are you going to do with the money? How much do you need? Do you know what you are getting into? Do you have the time and expertise to succeed? Do you need any help with your business venture? Will we get our money back, when and how much?
- What issues need to be addressed in the financing agreement? (what does everyone do)
- Think of ways to structure a financing deal (how to make it work)

Ways to finance:

- Borrow money from family or friends
- Use your savings
- Earn the money from doing odd jobs
- Attract investment from an investor

Please see our Chapter 12, "Additional Resources To Help You" section.

Budgeting

Budgeting is a process that businesses go through to plan their revenues and expenses. There are also more complicated capital budgets (purchase of assets) and cash flow budgets.

A budget is a quantitative statement (numbers or values or dollars) for revenues and expenses that are planned to happen in a business.
Budgeting of revenues helps a business make plans for things such as staffing requirements and materials to produce the product.
Every business needs to control its expenses (costs) to use its money wisely. By taking the time to budget (estimate) expenses, businesses will naturally go through the thinking process of whether expenses are necessary and if the costs are reasonable. Another important part of the budget process is determining the best price for these items and where to purchase them.

Apply to a lemonade stand or your business of choice

Give some thought to the level of sales you may achieve.

- Examine your traffic flow report to help you estimate your sales
- Look at past experience of your business or other businesses
- Prepare a summary of your estimated sales (by day, by week, by year)

Sales/Revenue Budget

Date	Comments	Planned Units Sold	Planned Selling Price Per Unit	Total Sales
August week 1	2 days	80	1.00	$ 80.00
August week 2	3 days	120	1.00	$120.00

This can be done by day, if you are only opening for a few days.

You will need to list and calculate the costs of all the items you require to run your business.

- What items do you need to run your business?
- How much are you planning on spending to get your business started?
- What are the expenses of running the business?

Example of an expense budget:

(A)	(B)	(C)	(D)	(E) = (B) x (D)
List your expenses	Quantity	Unit of measure	Cost per unit	Total Cost
Lemons	50	Lemon	0.15	$7.50
Sugar	1	1 lb. Bag	3.00	$3.00
Pad of paper				
Advertising				
Promotion				
Cups				
Other				
Total				

Money Management

Money management covers the way you take in and handle money. This includes how you take money from your customers, where you put your money, how you pay your bills and how you pay people you owe money to.

Businesses need to make sure the money they take in is safe and managed properly. Businesses have to be aware of the costs of managing their money and the benefits of paying off debt, earning interest from investments and other ways they can use their money.

Businesses need to make sure the money they earn is not lost or risked by putting it in places it can be lost or stolen. You also need to make sure you have controls to ensure the money your business receives, gets to the bank. If you sell 100 units of your product and the selling price is $1.00, you need to have controls to make sure the $100.00 is received and put in the bank. If your cash sales do not balance with your bank deposit, you need to be able to reconcile (figure out) the difference.

Apply to a lemonade stand or your business of choice

Treat the money you take in very carefully and make sure you use it wisely.

In your lemonade stand business you will need a float of money to make change. You need to be prepared in case your first few customers make their purchase with big bills or if you are selling your lemonade for 50 cents and everyone has dollars.

- How will you handle your money at the stand? (In a box, a cup) How much money will you keep at your stand?
- Where do you plan to put the money you make from your business? (ie. In the bank, your piggy bank, etc.)
- How do you know how much money you should take in based on the sales you have? What controls do you have that will ensure that the money from your sales of 20 glasses at 0.50 is in your moneybox?
- When and how do you plan to pay back the people you owe money to?
- How will you use the money you make in your business? (Save, invest back into your business, buy stuff, save for your education, contribute to your household, donate to charity or pay your debts etc.)

Payment Terms

This is a good opportunity for you to be creative with how you collect money. You can learn to take some risks and test alternative strategies.

Payment terms are the agreed way in which a buyer pays the seller for goods. Examples are cash, cheques, credit cards, credit payment in 30 days, etc.

This is about providing alternative ways for customers to pay for a product or service they buy. If a customer comes to a business with a cheque to buy a product and the business doesn't accept cheques, then there will not be a sale. A cash only plan will prevent many customers from buying from a business.

In business it is important to provide payment terms that allow you to attract sales while ensuring that you collect the money due to you. Businesses have to decide on payment terms that customers prefer and which the business can collect and make money on. If you allow customers to pay you in 60 or 90 days, you will have to make sure you collect the money and have the money to pay for bills during this time period. As you are considering the payment terms with your customers, you must also consider the payment terms you will have with your suppliers and the amount of cash and credit you have available.

When a business provides more payment terms for customers, this should lead to more product sales. Businesses have to figure out what terms customers need to do business with, how they can provide the payment terms, how to collect the money and how to make a reasonable profit with the terms.

Apply to a lemonade stand or your business of choice

In general, the lemonade stand business is a cash only business with little concern on when and if you will receive your money. Keep in mind you may increase your sales if you offer credit payment terms. A customer you know and trust may not have the money on them, but you believe they will pay you later. Offering payment terms of one day could make the difference of a sale or no sale.

Keep in mind, once you offer payment terms you take the risk of not collecting the money and having to take your losses. You will have to learn how to assess customers and determine who to give credit to.

- What type of payment should you accept for your product?
- What are the costs of each and how will your business benefit?
- Who should get credit? (Allow customers to pay later) Consider a "credit rating" for customers (ability to pay based on information you have)
- Make sure you determine how you are going to get paid. For cash sales, make sure you get paid before the person is given their product
- Examples of payment terms:

- Cash - what size of bills do you accept -will you accept $50.00 bills?
- IOU - I owe you – will pay you later
- Cheques - be careful accepting cheques – if the cheque is returned N.S.F. (non sufficient funds) the bank will charge you a significant service charge for processing the cheque and you won't get your money
- Barter - trade for another product or service. You can be very creative and have lots of fun with bartering - A glass of my lemonade is worth your best baseball card!
- Credit cards, bankcards etc.
- Credit of x days to pay
- PayPal or other e-mail money transfers. Interesting opportunity to pre-sell your product
- Consider receiving an e-mail payment and then having the person come and pick-up their product or have it delivered to them

Accounting

Accounting is the principles or practice of systematically recording, presenting and interpreting financial accounts. It is keeping track of money and transactions such as sales, expenses, assets, liabilities and equity.

For any business to be successful, it needs to handle its money, sales, expenses, assets, liabilities and equity in an organized fashion. Transactions or business dealings need to be recorded (written down or entered into a computer) in an organized and systematic way so that it is easy to find and use the information to manage the business.

Accounting has to be accurate, timely and most importantly, truthful. It is very important for any business, especially a public company owned by shareholders, to provide the confidence in their accounting records. The way to ensure confidence is to make sure the accounting is done using the proper guidelines and the people preparing the accounting records are only motivated to do a proper job.

Apply to a lemonade stand or your business of choice

- How are you going to keep track of the money so you can pay your bills and know how much money you are actually making?
- Keep a file with all the receipts for the items you bought

- If you obtained items from your kitchen at no cost to you, you should find out what they should have cost you and record these costs (you actually owe money for these items)
- Prepare a listing of all of the items used and the costs on a sheet of paper. Let's call this an expense ledger. Expense is an accounting term for costs

Figure out your total costs/expenses.

Example of an expense ledger to track your expenses:

(A) Date	(B) Name of Item	(C) Category	(D) Quantity Used	(E) Cost/per Quantity	(F) = (D) x (E) Total Expense
August 12	Lemons	Product Costs	50	0.15	7.50
August 12	Sign – paper	Advertising	1	1.50	1.50
August 12	Marker	Advertising	1	0.75	0.75

Keep track of your sales/revenues on your sales ledger to determine your daily sales and total sales.

Example of a sales ledger:

(A) Date	(B) Category of Sale	(C) Quantity Sold	(D) Selling Price	(E) = (C) x (D) Total Sales
August 12	Lemonade – large	40	$1.00	$40.00
August 12	Lemonade – small	20	0.50	$10.00

Once you have recorded your sales and expenses there are several steps you need to take to figure out your profit (how much money you are making):

- Your profit can be calculated by a simple math equation. Profit = Total Sales – Total Expenses
- Add up the "Total Expense" column from your expense ledger to determine how much your operations cost you
- Add up your "Total Sales" on your sales ledger. Sales are the amount of money you received.
- The difference between the "Total Sales" (revenues) and the "Total Expenses" (costs) equals your profit. Revenues – Expenses = Profit

Advanced Accounting

If you had costs to build a lemonade stand, then your accounting becomes a little more complicated.

If you are only going to use the lemonade stand once, then all of these costs should be included on your expense ledger. If the lemonade stand is used more than once, than the cost of it should be divided equally between times you used it. If you plan to use it twice, the costs should be allocated equally to these two periods. This accounting concept is called "depreciation of an asset". The concept is an asset (building, machinery or lemonade stand) has an economic life or a period of time it will be used. The cost of the asset should be spread over the life of the asset. If your lemonade stand is expected to last for and be used for two years, then the costs should be shown on your accounting records for the two years.

Why does this matter? If you sold $50.00 of lemonade and your supplies or expenses are $30.00, you would think you made a profit of $20.00. But, if your lemonade stand cost you $20.00 to make and you planned to use it once, then you would have broke even or made no money. ($50.00 revenue - $30.00 expenses - $20.00 depreciation = $0.00 breakeven)

If you sold another $60.00 the next time you operated your lemonade stand and had expenses of $36.00, you would have a profit before depreciation of $24.00. If the lemonade stand were to be used twice, your depreciation would be $20.00/2 or $10.00. Therefore, you would make a profit after depreciation of:
Day one: $50.00 (revenue) -$30.00 (expenses) -$10.00 (depreciation) =$10.00
Day two: $60.00 (revenue) -$36.00 (expenses) -$10.00 (depreciation) = $14.00

Chapter 11

Other Important Business Considerations

In This Chapter

Environmental Considerations
External Factors
Charity – Philanthropy
Mergers
Acquisitions
Franchising
Partnerships
Business Law
Regulations
The End Of DAB

Environmental Considerations

Environmental considerations are things that affect the environment around you. As our environment continues to suffer from pollution, we all need to contribute to a solution to stop/reduce pollution. Recycling, reusing and conserving are very helpful ways to help the environment.

Many businesses provide educational programs to help people understand environmental issues and opportunities to get involved and take action. Many businesses also do research and development to change their products and processes to make them more energy efficient, use recycled materials or use less materials.

Apply to a lemonade stand or your business of choice

To be environmentally responsible you need to consider a number of things:

- Research the possible harm your business could cause to the environment
- Do you have an environmental friendly business plan?
- Do you use reusable glasses or recyclable glasses?
- Do you recycle things that you used to make your lemonade? (ie. Compost lemons skins)
- Have you taken the appropriate steps to ensure your customers do not pollute the neighbourhood with your product?
- Have you created communications material for your customers and employees on what your business is doing for the environment?

External Factors

External factors relate to things that can happen outside of your business, but will affect your business.

External factors have to be taken into account for all businesses since they can't control everything that goes on around them. For example:

- What if something happens in your area attracting lots of people – like the Olympics
- A business can advertise to attract customers, but what happens if the TV station airing the advertising goes out of business or has a fire? Your planned advertisements will not be shown
- What happens if there is a shortage of good water supply to make a product?
- What happens if the government changes regulations to prevent a business from providing its product?

Apply to lemonade stand

- Many factors outside of your control, such as weather, will affect your business. Watch the weather forecast and alter your days and hours of operation based on weather conditions. If the forecast calls for hot weather, this could help your business and you should plan for a busier time. If the forecast is rain, you may consider closing the stand that day

- Another key external factor may be a major event happening in your area. This could be a garage sale, a fair or parade, which could all contribute to increased opportunities for your business
- List external factors that could affect your business. Think of a back-up plan (contingency plan) - what would I do if these situations happened?

Charity - Philanthropy

Charity is a desire to help mankind by giving gifts (often money) to charitable or humanitarian institutions. Charity is also giving money and resources to non-profit organizations or giving to help other people.

There are many good things that charities do such as helping kids in need. Charities tend to rely on the generosity of volunteers who work for free to help advance their cause. Donations from people and businesses provide charities with money to provide the services to people who need their help.

Most people try and help others in some way and a charity is a common way of doing it. You can usually find a charity that is working on something you are interested in, or that needs your help.

It is a good business practice to make an effort to help charities in your community. Customers tend to respect and do business with companies that care about the issues they care about and which support the community the business operates in. People tend to want to work for companies that support charities and take an interest in their community.

Apply to a lemonade stand or your business of choice

- Identify charities you would be interested in supporting
- How can your business help other people?
- How can you help other people?
- Have you considered using some of your profits to benefit charity?

- How much of your proceeds will you give to charity and to which charities? Consider a percentage of your profits or an amount per unit of product sold
- Consider having a charity day proceeds from your business are used to benefit charity
- Consider providing opportunities for kids from a youth group to help at your stand
- Consider sharing this book with other kids

Mergers

This is an area that you can have lots of fun discussing and dreaming about.
Mergers are the combining of businesses to create a larger business that is managed jointly by the two businesses that merged.

Mergers tend to happen in business, because there are advantages of being a bigger team and working together.

In theory, a company that has the expertise in a particular business could easily transfer that expertise to a larger company. As a larger company, there is often a greater opportunity to grow and succeed.

As many businesses are expanding internationally, there tends to be lots of merger activity. A bank that operates in one country will have difficulty opening new banks in other countries. A merger strategy with a bank in another country will allow both of the banks to be involved in banking in other countries.

Apply to a lemonade stand or your business of choice

Use this as an opportunity to talk to other business kids about combining your businesses. Think through the idea of having one group make the lemonade, one group building and maintaining the stands, a group in charge of advertising and group in charge of sales. Each of the individual businesses may have a strength that will benefit from a larger group of businesses.

- Should you merge with another business in your area?
- Examine mergers in other businesses and try and determine why they merged and what they need to do to succeed. Try and understand why one industry is merging and apply it to your industry and your business.

- Should you explore merger opportunities in other areas? (Neighbourhoods, cities or countries)

Acquisitions

Acquisitions are an advanced business practice, but it is something you should consider.

Acquisitions is acquiring or being acquired. An acquisition occurs when one company buys another company.

Acquisitions are often done to quickly expand a company's business through a purchase of another company rather then developing a business internally.

It is often done to diversify a company so that its profits are not dependant on one type of business. A summer time business may acquire a wintertime business so they have a year round business. Therefore, this business is not reliant on one season.

Businesses can be targets for acquisition if they are not being managed well or performing as well as they could.

Apply to a lemonade stand or your business of choice

If you feel you can raise the money to buy a business, manage to grow it and make it more profitable, you should consider an acquisition. If you don't acquire a business you can still go through the process of figuring out if you should, what price to pay and how to manage it.

- Should you buy a lemonade stand business from someone else?
- Is there a lemonade stand business you feel you can buy for a good price and run it differently to make it more successful?
- Do you want to expand your lemonade stand business by acquiring other stands? Do you feel you can manage additional sites?
- Is there another business you would be interested in buying?
- Do you have the financing and the management team available to acquire a business?

Franchising

Can you imagine being the McDonald's of lemonade stands! Your stands could be all over the world serving your lemonade from a stand similar to yours.

To franchise is to take a successful way of doing business and to sell it to other people so they can copy the successful methods and expand it in other areas. People purchase franchise rights to operate similar business operations in other areas. For example, McDonald's is a franchise.

People that buy franchise rights believe a franchise business with a proven success record will give them a better chance of succeeding in business. In return for the payment of franchise rights and royalties (a percentage of the sales), you get access to experienced & sophisticated business operators who buy things at a better price, make important business decisions, provide support and oversee the success of the business.

As a number of franchises pay rights fees and fund advertising campaigns, the franchising company has more money and bargaining power to advertise and develop the business. This is a competitive advantage over smaller individual businesses.

Apply to a lemonade stand or your business of choice

- Is your lemonade stand business format (way you do business) ready for franchising?
- Have you demonstrated success and do you have a look and approach that can be copied and sold?
- Could you sell your approach and coach others on running a lemonade stand?
- Could you mange the growth of your type of lemonade stand in other neighbourhoods, cities and countries?
- Are you able to buy all the things required for other lemonade stands and deliver them to the stands?
- Look at franchises and figure out why they can franchise their businesses. Learn from their mistakes and successes. Check out their web sites
- Look at franchise information packages to learn what they are doing. Consider how they mange their business, advertisements, etc
- Develop your own franchise package to try and attract interest from other kids
- Go to a franchise show and see how other franchisers are approaching the franchising of their business

- Examine franchise magazines for ideas
- Do some brainstorming on what a lemonade stand franchise should be

Partnerships

You have made friends to do a variety of things together. You have friends from sports teams, school and other things you are involved in. You are likely to become friendly with people who share similar interests. Business partnerships evolve as friends with similar interests or as a team of people with a variety of skills needed to make a business succeed. A business partnership is a legal arrangement between people to work together as a team and share the responsibilities and risks of the business. It is a formal arrangement to work with someone.

Partnerships are used in business to bring people together with different skills to work as partners to develop and operate a business. There is usually a greater chance of success when you have good partners with different skills to share the work and obligations of the business.

If you were to approach a partner for your business, you would want to be clear on what each of you would do, how you would share responsibilities, the amount of money you would put into the business and how you would share the profits.

You should appreciate that partnerships may not work, just as music bands break up for various reasons. It is important to choose your partner wisely and make sure that you can work together and that you share similar values and goals.

Apply to a lemonade stand or your business of choice

- Should you work with a partner?
- Who might your partner(s) be?

How should your partnership share the following?

- The responsibilities of developing and running the business
- The money required to get started
- The profit the business makes
- The business decisions necessary to run the business. How should your partnership decide on pricing, location, design, etc?

- How does a partner leave the partnership and how do you settle the allocation of money and things of value (assets) in the business?

Business Law

Kids are well aware of rules and businesses have many rules too. Business rules have been created through the development of laws, which are enforced in our legal system.

Business law is conducting business within the rules of law. Business decisions have to be considered within the rules of law and should be guided by policies and procedures, or be referred to legal council (a lawyer) for advice.

Businesses in general have many legal issues to deal with. Legal considerations start with the set-up of the business, hiring of people, buying & selling of products, business agreements, collecting money, financing and legal disputes, etc. There are laws for each of these business decisions.

Intellectual Properties is an interesting area that requires legal expertise for copyrights (©) and trademarks (® or ™). This book is copyright protected to prevent it from being illegally copied. Product names and word phrases or slogans are trademarked to prevent their unauthorized use. Companies should take the appropriate legal steps to register and protect their original ideas.

Apply to a lemonade stand or your business of choice

Hopefully you will not have legal issues at your stand but you should anticipate potential legal matters and include them in your plan.

- If you develop an amazing name for your product, you should ™ it which is giving it a trademark
- If your lemonade recipe is original, you should consider protecting the recipe with © to protect it from being copied by other people
- If your business is a huge success and you want to expand it, then you may consider using a lawyer to register an appropriate company name and set-up a proper company structure

- You may want to TM your advertising slogan to protect others from using your original phrase
- Look for lawyers in your telephone book or through web site searches. Read their advertisements and view their web sites to understand how your business could use their services
- Try the "If I had this problem, what would I do?" game

Regulations

Regulations are laws by which you must conduct business. Regulations are rules you must abide by.

It is important for governments and associations to develop and enforce laws for businesses. Laws are necessary to ensure consumers are protected and businesses operate in a responsible way. If businesses could make money with no regulation, there may not be any concern for other issues such as people's safety and the environment.

Apply to a lemonade stand or your business of choice

- Are there by-laws, zoning laws or regulations controlling business in your area?
- Do you need permits or some type of license to sell lemonade or to run a business?
- Does your product need to be certified or inspected?
- Do your employees need to be a certain age or paid a minimum wage?
- What regulations do you think your business should have?
- How do you think regulations should be enforced?
- Research regulations for business and see how they apply to your business

The End of DAB

Hopefully, this was an interesting and challenging experience for you.

Congratulations! Working through this guide is a major accomplishment! Before this guide, not many kids have actually sat down and gone through the process of developing a business. Make sure to include this experience on your résumé.

You have now gone through the steps to develop a business. This is a good time to celebrate, take a break, reflect on your business and at some point in time, go back and further develop your business. This is not a test where you have one chance at doing it. You will make mistakes, change your mind and realize you want to try different approaches to your business. This is expected, and you should do what you have to do to develop a business you are satisfied with.

The exciting part of finishing DAB is that you will feel confident to apply what you have learned to other business opportunities. The end of this experience will lead to the beginning of others.

Chapter 12

Additional Resources To Help You In Business

In This Chapter

Kid's Business Contest
Web Site Resources
Inspiration From Anecdotes
Editorials On Kids And Business
Business Case Of The Lemonade Stand
How Do You Teach Kids Business? – With "How Was Your Day?"
Kid's Business Club Guide
Brainstorming Tips
Press Release – Repositioning The Lemonade Stand
Business Plan Framework
Business Terminology or Dictionary
Kid's Business Club Guide
Brainstorming Tips
Press Release – Repositioning The Lemonade Stand
Business Plan Framework
Business Terminology or Dictionary
Closing Comments

Kid's Business Contest

Framework To Consider For A Contest:

The following information is recommended:

- Pictures - photos or your drawings of your lemonade stand. We are very interested in the creativity of your lemonade stand design – what materials did you used to build your lemonade stand?
- Product – recipe you chose, how you made the lemonade
- Services – what services did you provide beyond your lemonade product?
- Advertisements and promotional - how did you let people know about your lemonade stand?
- Selling approach – what did/would you say to people to get them to buy your lemonade?
- Customer satisfaction – testimonial from customers – what your customers thought about your lemonade stand, what customers think of your service and your lemonade
- Team – people that helped you – team members - what did each person do?
- Business plans – the steps you took to get organized and to set-up your lemonade stand, the location you chose, all the decisions you had to make to get started
- Performance – how long were you in business? How much did you sell? How many people passed by? How many stopped at your stand? How many purchased your lemonade?

Contest to participate in:

If you would like to participate in a contest see www.teachingkidsbusiness.com/lemonade-stand-contest.htm. This page name may change, so go to www.teachingkidsbusiness.com and find the current link.

Do research on entrepreneurial awards.

Web Site Resources

www.TheKidsGuideToBusiness.com
We have created book updates and links to additional business programming. Check out **our Kids Business Rewards Program for discounts and additional business programming.**

www.teachingkidsbusiness.com/lemonade-stand.htm
This online program provides links to resources, which will help you learn about business and plan/develop a lemonade stand business.

www.teachingkidsbusiness.com/seed-capital-financing.htm
Seed Capital Program to help you finance your business venture.

www.teachingkidsbusiness.com/business-basics.htm
This program is a kid-friendly introduction to business basics.

www.teachingkidsbusiness.com/entrepreneurship-program.htm
This program is an introduction to entrepreneurship for kids. It has several entrepreneurial stories to help you understand how to develop an entrepreneurial idea.

www.teachingkidsbusiness.com/kids-works-ventures.htm
Explore commercial opportunities for kids' works.

www.kidse-marketplace.com
When you are ready for an entrepreneurial venture (creating your own product and business) you will be given the opportunity to launch a kid's business online in a kids' marketplace.

www.teachingkidsbusiness.com/kids-business-e-store.htm
The Kids' Business e-store has been created to provide unique business related products for kids. "The kid's Gift of Business™" is about giving kids an opportunity to have a business experience. The uniqueness of these gifts is they are kid-friendly business products, can be enjoyed now, throughout a number of years and can influence a child's future.

Please note that as the TeachingKidsBusiness.com web site grows, the page names for the programs may change. If you have problems with the above web pages, please go to www.teachingkidsbusiness.com and find the appropriate link from the home page or other sections.

Inspiration From Anecdotes

You can read this area to help inspire yourself and others, to do your best and to challenge yourself to be the best you can. Kind words help motivate people.

"If we all did the things we are capable of doing, we would literally astound ourselves."
Thomas Edison

"Business, a game kids can play™!"
Jeff Brown, Founder of TeachingKidsBusiness.com

"The journey of a thousand miles begins with one step."
Lao-Tsu

"Entrepreneurs are simply those who understand that there is little difference between obstacle and opportunity and are able to turn both to their advantage."
Victor Kiam

"Inspiration is the feeling I get when I hear the pride in my mom's voice when I tell her about something I have accomplished."
Sameer Zaman

"Only those who dare to fail greatly can ever achieve greatly."
Robert F. Kennedy

"If I believe I cannot do something, it makes me incapable of doing it. But when I believe I can, then I acquire the ability to do it, even if I did not have the ability in the beginning."
Mahatma Gandhi

"Do what you do so well that when other people see what it is that you do, they will want to see you do it again... and they will bring others with them to show them what it is that you do."
Walt Disney

"Imagination is more important than knowledge."
Albert Einstein

"She didn't know it couldn't be done so she went ahead and did it."
Mary's Almanac

"A smart businessperson is one who makes a mistake, learns from it, and never makes it again. A wise businessperson is one who finds a smart business person and learns from him how to avoid the mistakes he made."
Jim Abrams

"Try a thing you haven't done three times. Once, to get over the fear of doing it. Twice, to learn how to do it. And a third time, to figure out whether you like it or not."
Virgil Thomson

"Failure is success if we learn from it."
Malcolm Forbes

"A determined soul will do more with a rusty monkey wrench than a loafer will accomplish with all the tools in a machine shop."
Rupert Hughes

"People are not lazy. They simply have impotent goals - that is, goals that do not inspire them."
Anthony Robbins

"Play experience can prepare the student for purposefulness in non-play activities, for true play creates the incentive to use one's best ability."
Neva Boyd

"Go confidently in the direction of your dreams. Live the life you have imagined."
Henry David Thoreau

"The people who get on in this world are the people who get up and look for the circumstances they want, and if they can't find them, make it."
George Bernard Shaw

"The will to win is useless without the will to prepare."
Henry David Thoreau

"I learned that a great leader is a man who has the ability to get other people to do what they don't want to do and like it."
Harry S. Truman

"Genius is one percent inspiration, and ninety-nine percent perspiration."
Thomas Edison

"There are three things extremely hard: steel, a diamond, and to know one's self."
Benjamin Franklin

"When you find your passion or your drive, it's like you're not doing it to be successful or to make some money. You love all those additional things that happen. But you're doing it because that's what you love. It gets you up early and it keeps you up late. You notice things. You have an impact and you have a sense of contribution. And life is really joyous."
Tony Robbins

"It is more important to do the right thing than to do the thing right."
Peter F. Drucker

"What we label speculation when we lose, becomes an investment when we win."
Far East Fortune Cookie Co. Ltd

Business Case of the Lemonade Stand

The lemonade stand is one of the most recognizable businesses in North America, that generates revenues in many markets, creates many jobs and puts a whole new face on business.

We know these businesses exist, we know that they are run by eager and talented young professionals and most of us would stop and gladly patronize a lemonade stand.

Is this where the KISS (keep it simple stupid) principles of business came from? As many MBA and other business programs teach business case studies, why have they never considered such a simple and successful business case?

The people that develop these ventures are true entrepreneurs. They inspire us all and they make many people proud. They have a passion for what they are doing and they overcome many obstacles to make their ventures work. They are a success by their experiences alone and very refreshing to see in business.

We should all take lessons on business from these amazing business leaders who operate lemonade stands.

By: Jeff Brown
Founder of TeachingKidsBusiness.com

How Do You Teach Kids Business? ™ - With "How Was Your Day?"

Have you ever responded to the question, "How was your day?" with "not bad" or "ok" or "terrible" or "I don't want to talk about it." Have you asked your child the same question and got a very vague answer like " ok". Have you ever got the answer of "stuff" when you ask your child "what they did at school today?" As a child, did you ever give the same type of response?

From our own personal experiences we can confidently say there is room for improvement on the "How was your day?" routine. We could actually use it as an opportunity to connect with one another, share a little guidance and get a little more involved in what is happening in their lives. We could find out what is important to them and use the discussion as an opportunity to lead into other conversations.

You may want to consider some "take it to the next level" ideas:

- A great starting point is to assume the role of listener, so that the child recognizes you are listening and interested in what they have to say. Nod your head and make some acknowledging sounds like – "really", "that's neat" or maybe even a "wow" or "cool" or whatever the current term is.
- Do not be so quick to pass judgment because that is probably the quickest way to end the conversation.

When you get the very vague answer like "stuff", try and ask what kind of stuff and have a little fun with it. Your child will learn to explain a situation and develop an opinion. Try and relate what they have to say to your world, your day or even a similar experience you had as a kid. This will help them form a perspective on the world around them and most importantly, to put things in perspective.

 Throughout your conversations, try and find some positive points. Try and relate the conversation to their future and possibly how it is handled in business. In the case of a problem, help them arrive at a solution or provide advice on how things could be handled.

Use a small part of this time to talk about something you saw today, since it will help them form a perspective on their surroundings. Talk about how well you were served at lunch, an interesting fashion, or an advertisement that caught your eye. Try and think in terms of business through the eyes of a child or in a way they can connect.

There are many interesting things to talk about when you are asked, "How was your day?" and it can be a launching pad for lots of other good things to talk about. It may be hard to get started, therefore be creative and patient.

By: Jeff Brown
Founder of TeachingKidsBusiness.com

Kid's Business Club Guide

Here is a framework for starting a business club:

1. Make a list of people you think might be interested in joining a business club and becoming part of your business team.
2. For your business club, write out how often you plan to meet and how you plan to develop and discuss your business.
3. Ask the people from your list if they are interested in joining a business club, when they would be available, if they know someone else that might be interested, and other things that are important to them. Make sure the way you plan to run the business club is okay with the other members.
4. Once you have some interested people, plan your starting meeting (set a one page agenda with a list of the things you want to discuss), communicate it to everyone (give them a copy of the agenda) and set a date to get together. The first meeting can be about reviewing the book and discussing some initial ideas on developing a lemonade stand business.
5. When you get together, figure out how best to work together (team work). Trial and error may be the best approach. Try one approach and see how it works. There is no right or wrong approach as it depends on the people in the club. You will start to discover management theories on how to run your meetings and your business.
6. You may want to have each member put in $5.00 to $10.00 to cover expenditures you may need for supplies or research resources.
7. When you meet, don't loose sight that it is not a dinner party or something the host has to spend a lot of money on. Keep it simple and even have members bring a snack. You can also have quick meetings at school, on the phone, e-mail or in chat rooms.
8. Each time you get together, go through a section in The Kids' Guide To Business. You can break off in teams and address certain areas. If necessary assign job responsibilities that should be done before the next meeting.

Brainstorming Tips

Brainstorming is a great way to come up with ideas. The goal of brainstorming is to come up with a long list of "crazy ideas". Brainstorming gets people to think in ways they don't normally think. It is important to have fun and not criticize (don't say, "what a stupid idea"). The basic rules are:

1. Quantity, not quality (more is better) is important to generate as many ideas as possible and don't worry how good they are at this stage.

2. No ideas can be criticized and no idea is too wild to write down. Remember, they are all good ideas at this stage.

3. It doesn't matter who came up with the idea first, work together to build on it and generate more ideas.

You may find that it is hard to come up with ideas on your own. It's okay to get a little help. Try and get a group of friends or family members together, to brainstorm some ideas. Here are some helpful tips:

- Start telling everyone what you would like him or her to think about
- Have each person write down as many ideas as he or she can think of, on individual pieces of paper
- Share the ideas with the group by having each person read their ideas aloud to the group, or by having one person read them all
- Have a question and answer period, where people can ask about the ideas that were presented and have the person that came up with the idea explain it to make sure everyone understands it
- Have a vote for the best idea. You can vote by raising your hands, or by having everyone write down their favourite idea and add up the results

Press Release - Repositioning The Lemonade Stand

Press Release - For Immediate Release
TeachingKidsBusiness.com
November 25, 2002

Jeff Brown, Founder of TeachingKidsBusiness.com is very pleased to provide kids with a lemonade stand program to help launch kids into business, to teach kids about business and to create a low risk impactful business experience.

The Lemonade Stand is a symbol of entrepreneurship and kids beginning in business. It has lasted for generations and all indications are, that it will thrive in the future. But all business models need to evolve and adapt to the changing marketplace. In this case, the changes can occur with some simple tips and a little coaching for these dynamic entrepreneurs.

Brown created the program with " goals to revitalize and enhance the lemonade stand experience. A venture of this nature is a great opportunity to introduce kids not only to basic business, but to also introduce more sophisticated business disciplines. Just a little extra thinking and planning will add dramatically to the lemonade stand experience."

We have taken for granted that kids are eager to go into the lemonade stand business, but do we appreciate the impact that it can have on kids. Traditionally the focus has been with kids, 10 and under, but this program positions the lemonade stand to be an excellent challenge and learning experience for kids of any age. By providing some basic business guidelines, the lemonade stand program can now be used by older kids. The experience can be just a business planning experience, creating a business case or a full-blown business launch.

Brown states that, "As you try and mirror the business aspects of other businesses, you will realize that a lemonade stand business can become quite a complex business case and therefore a great business challenge for kids."

This kids' lemonade stand program can be found at www.teachingkidsbusiness.com/lemonade-stand.htm. TeachingKidsBusiness.com is developing to engage and inspire kids at an early age (8 and up) to develop confidence, experience, and business skills and explore career choices. The web site presents "tools", "experiences" and "community involvement" support in a safe, educational, non-pressure, non-commercial and fun way.

For more information, go to the web site at www.teachingkidsbusiness.com, email us at: info@teachingkidsbusiness.com, or contact Jeff Brown directly, by phoning 999-999-9999.

Business Plan Framework

You don't have to actually go through this section and write a business plan, but we would like you to get a basic understanding of what a business plan should cover.

A business plan is a document summarizing what a business plans to do and how it is going to be done. The plan covers the present and future strategy for developing the business and its financial position.

The plan is usually presented as follows:

Cover Page: Business name and contact information.

1. Table of Contents: This section provides a detailed summary of the plan by title and page number.
2. Executive Summary: This is usually a two-page document that summarizes what is in the plan. This allows a reader to quickly understand what the plan is all about. The executive summary should include information on the company, the product, the target market, and the strategy of pursuing the market, when and how you will complete the plan and what you want the reader to do for you.
3. The Company: This is an opportunity to talk about the direction the company is taking.
4. The Team: Who is going to make it happen?
5. The Product: This section is to talk about your product and explain its main features and benefits.
6. The Market: This section should talk about who is going to buy your product.
7. Marketing Plan: This should explain how you are going to introduce your product, promote and sell it.
8. Key Issues: All businesses are faced with issues, which need to be overcome to succeed. You need to consider all possible obstacles that my face your business and provide a solution.
9. Financial Statements: You need to write out your plan in terms of money. All the decisions you make will cost money and should help the company make money.

Business Terminology or Dictionary

You need to know a language to communicate with people whether it is a different culture or industry; business has a language of its own. Here, we have provided the terms and definitions that are commonly used in business. For anyone to start into business they need to understand the basics of business which includes the language or terms in business.

We have created this "Business Terminology Section" to provide you with business terms and a kid-friendly translation. As you learn the language of business you will understand how to think and communicate in business terms. As you learn to think in business terms you will begin to use frameworks or guidelines to help you work through business related issues and opportunities. As you learn to communicate in business you will be able to get your message out to customers, other businesses and organizations.

Here are basic business terms:

Advertising
Advertising is a communication that is paid for by an identified sponsor with the object of promoting ideas, goods, or services. Advertising includes any printed or broadcast message that is sent and paid for by an identified organization to a target market via television, radio, newspapers, magazines, direct mail, billboards, web site banners and transit cards etc.

Balance sheet
It is a summary statement (report) of accounting values of assets (things you own - bike); liabilities (money you owe - borrowed money); stock (ownership in the company) and retained earnings (assets less liabilities)

Blue sky
This refers to laws that protect investors from being misled by investment people who misrepresent (lie about) the value of investments to trick people into taking their money.

Barter

Barter is a method of trading in which goods and services are exchanged without the use of money.

You may want to accept things other then money for your lemonade product. A customer might have an extra trading card they would be willing to exchange for lemonade.

Brainstorming

Brainstorming is a group discussion in order to invoke ideas and solve business problems. No idea is rejected, no matter how irrelevant it appears, until it has been thoroughly discussed.

As you work through the many things to think about in planning your lemonade stand, you should use brainstorming.

Brand (brand name)

A brand is a name, term, symbol, or design that is intended to clearly identify and differentiate a seller's product from the products of his or her competitors. A brand name is used to identify a specific product.

You will want to consider choosing a brand name for your lemonade to help people distinguish your product from others. Your product is not just lemonade!

Brand extension

Using a successful brand name to launch a new or modified product in a separate category. A successful brand helps businesses enter new product categories more easily. Example: A lemonade frozen product like a Popsicle would be a brand extension from your lemonade.

Burnout

A work-related condition of emotional exhaustion in which interest in work, personal achievement, and efficiency decline sharply and the sufferer is no longer capable of making decisions.

Be careful, this could happen to you and your associates if you put too much time in the operating of your business. Keep yourself fresh (the same goes for your product).

Business

Business is a trade, a profession, a person's usual occupation, the buying and selling or trade and a commercial firm or a shop. Business is really as simple as coming up with a product or service and finding a way for people to buy it from you.

Business Analysis
Business analysis is to evaluate a businesses performance. How is your business doing? After you have been in business for a while (this could be minutes, hours or days) take a look at your business and think about how you could do things better.

Business Plan
A business plan is a document summarizing what a business plans to do and how it plans to do it. The plan covers the company's present and future strategy for developing the business and its financial position.

Business Process Re-Engineering (BPR)
It is an examination of your business by first determining what the business is trying to achieve, what is its main activities and what things it does best. Then you come up with a plan to achieve your goals.
This is a good opportunity to act like a business consultant and step back and look at your own or other lemonade stand businesses.

Business Strategy
A business strategy is an overall strategy that coordinates functional areas of a business. It defines the business objectives, analyses the internal and external environments and determines the strategic direction of the firm.
For example, a business strategy to diversify into new markets would be accomplished by introducing new products to your business.

Business Structure
A business structure is the formal structure of a business. At the simplest level it is a sole-proprietor, which is a small business run by a single owner. A partnership is a business owned and controlled by two or more persons through a partnership agreement while a public company is a company structure where it is owned by many shareholders who own stock in the company.

Buy-back
The buying back by a company of its shares from its investors, who have put venture capital up for the formation of the company.

Cannibalization
A market situation in which increased sales of one-brand results in decreased sales of another brand with the same product line.

If you were to begin to sell apple juice at your lemonade stand, the sales of apple juice would cannibalize the sales of your lemonade. This is okay if you sell more drinks overall and if you make as much money selling apple juice as you do for lemonade.

Capacity

Capacity is the highest sustainable output from an operating system in units per given time. There is a capacity you have on how much lemonade you can possibly make and sell. If you have only one jug of lemonade and one pourer, your capacity is that jug and the time it takes you to pour it. If you have only one jug of lemonade available to your business then that is the capacity of your sales for the time period that you are in business. If you have the ability to make more product then your capacity is increased and so is your potential business.

Capital

Capital is the money that is contributed by the business owners to allow the business to function.

If you used $10.00 to get your lemonade stand started, then that is the amount of capital you put into your business.

Capital Gains

The gain on the disposal (sale) of an asset calculated by deducting the cost of the asset from the proceeds received from the disposal of the asset.
If you bought or developed your lemonade stand for a cost of $25.00 and sold it for $40.00, you would have a capital gain of $15.00.

Career

A career is the progress through life, especially in a profession, an occupation, and a way of making a living, especially one with opportunities for advancement or promotion. A career is the choice you make to earn a living, job or occupation.

Cartel

An association of independent companies formed to regulate the price and sales conditions of the product or services they offer.
If you got together with other lemonade stand operators and decided to set the pricing for lemonade in your area, you would be acting as a cartel. Be careful because setting prices and controlling supply is against the law in many countries.

Caveat

A caveat is a proviso or qualification that limits liability by putting another party on notice. For example, a retailer (lemonade stand) may sell goods subject to the caveat that no guarantee of their suitability for a particular purpose is given. The purchaser in these circumstances has no remedy against the retailer should the goods in fact turn out to be unsuitable for that particular purpose.

Caveat Emptor

(Latin: Let the buyer beware). This implies that the purchaser of goods must take care to ensure that they are free from defects of quality, fitness, or title. If the goods turn out to be defective, the purchaser has no remedy against the seller. This assumes that the purchaser has the opportunity to examine the goods.

Co-branding

An arrangement between two or more companies in which they agree to display joint content and perform joint promotions using brand logos or banner advertisements.

Cold Call

This refers to a selling technique in which a salesperson approaches a customer with little or no warning. You have probably received many cold calls on your telephone at home.

Collateral

This is an asset that is used to secure a loan. The asset would be taken from you in the event that you can't pay the loan back. If you were to borrow money to develop your lemonade stand business, your stand would probably be used as collateral. If you didn't pay the money back, the person who gave you the money would take the collateral (your stand would become theirs) as payment.

Commission

A payment made to, example a sales person, usually calculated as a percentage of the goods sold.
If you were to hire people to sell lemonade, you may look at paying them a commission for what they sell. If they sell $10.00 of lemonade and you give them a 10% commission, you would pay them $10.00 x 0.10 = $1.00.

Confidentiality Clause

A clause in a contract of employment that details types of information that an employee will acquire on joining the firm that may not be passed on to anyone outside of the firm.

A good example of this would be the information on how your lemonade is made. This should not be shared by any of your employees when they leave to go work at a stand down the street.

Someone could come and work for you and learn your recipe for your product and then leave your business and take your ideas and open up their own stand. This can be prevented with a confidentiality clause and legal enforcement.

Conglomerate

A conglomerate is diverse group of companies, which are usually managed by a holding company.

If you were to own a lemonade stand business, a grass cutting business, a painting business and dog walking business then you would be a conglomerate.

Copyright

A copyright is a legal proviso, indicating ownership of written or drawn material such that the material cannot be reproduced without the expressed consent of the author.

The Kids' Guide To Business is copyright by the writer.

Core Competency

A proficiency in a critical functional activity (making lemonade), such as technical know-how or a particular business specialization, that leads to providing a company's unique competitive advantage. Basically, this is what your business is good at.

Corporate Culture

Corporate culture is the values, beliefs, norms, and traditions within an organization that influence the behaviour of its members.

If you are friendly towards your customers, respective of their needs, fair to the people that work at your stand and provide a fast and courteous service, you will have created a good corporate culture.

Corporate Governance

Corporate governance is the manner in which an organization is managed and the nature of accountability of the managers to the owners. This is about how decisions are made in a business and how others accept the way decisions are made.

Corporate Image
The corporate image is the image (mental picture of something) that a company projects of itself. Is your business good to work for, are you honest, respectful, do you demonstrate a position on important things such as the environment, education, working conditions?

Corporation
A corporation is a type of business, a separate entity from those persons who run it. A corporation provides limited liability, easy transfer of ownership and unlimited life for a business.

Cost
Cost is an expenditure, usually of money, for the purchase of goods or services. The money you pay for your ingredients to make lemonade is a cost.

Credit
Credit is the reputation and financial standing of a person or organization.
If you pay your bills and money that you owe to people, you will develop good credit.

Credit Line
A credit line is a facility for borrowing money.
Banks usually provide this to businesses by giving them access to a certain amount of money, as they need it for their business. If you go to your parents and they agree to advance you money when your business needs money, they are basically giving you a line of credit.

Creditor
A creditor is one to whom an organization or person owes money.

Customer
Any individual, household, or company representative that acts as a buyer of goods and services offered to the mass market is a customer.

Customer Service
The services an organization offers to its customers. This covers a wide variety of services, including after-sales service, extended guarantees, regular mailings of information and telephone calls in case of complaints etc.

Any dealings you have with your customers should be considered customer service as you try to help and give them an excellent level of service to satisfy their needs and keep them happy.

DAB
Develop a Business. We have created this term to help kids focus on thinking about business by working towards developing a business. We consider developing a business to include the imagination of a business or actually creating a business.

Debt
The sum of money owed by one person to another.

Debt-Equity Ratio
A ratio used to examine the financial structure of a business. It is used in determining the borrowing level for a business.
Your goal should be to have zero debt with lots of equity. If you were to have $10.00 of debt with $2.00 of equity, you would have a 10/2 or 5:1 debt ratio. This means that you would have five times the amount of debt to the equity you have. It would be much better to have a 1:5 debt-equity ratio.

Development Stage
The stage in the development of a new product during which the concept is transformed into a prototype and the basic marketing strategy is developed.
The first time you make your lemonade and start testing it to see if it is good - this is your development stage. You will eventually need to decide on the product you will be selling at your stand.

Direct Marketing
Selling by means of dealing directly with consumers rather than through retailers. Methods include mail order, telephone selling, door-to-door calling, telemarketing, magazine and TV advertising and on-line computer shopping.
If you were to contact people in your neighbourhood about your lemonade business you would be applying direct marketing.

Disposable Income
It is the income a person has available to spend after paying income taxes, other taxes and other deductions payable to the government for employment income. It is the money that people have available to spend.

The key consideration for business is that their customers have enough disposable income to buy the products. If you are trying to do business where people don't have the money for your product, your business will not succeed.

Dollar
A dollar is the standard monetary unit of a number of countries such as Australia, Canada, Malaysia, Taiwan, the USA, Zimbabwe and others.
Depending on where you operate your business, you will need to determine the type of money that you will accept.

Doubtful Debts
Money owed to an organization, which it is unlikely to receive.
If you allow little Johnny to have a glass of lemonade even though he says he has no money and probably will not be able to pay for it later, you will have a doubtful debt.

Due Diligence
This refers to the investigation process an investor should conduct into the operations and business it wants to invest in. Before you buy stock in a company, you should do your homework on who is running the company and how well the company has done in the past, present and in the future.

Emotional Appeal
Emotional appeal is the attempt by advertising to stir up negative or positive emotions to motivate a purchase.
If you were to use an advertisement saying the proceeds from your lemonade stand would be going towards a college education, you could probably create some emotional appeal with people.

Empowerment
This is the giving of increased responsibility and a measure of control to employees in their working lives. The concept is based on the view that people need personal satisfaction and fulfilment in their work and that responsibility and control increase satisfaction.
You will get a sense of empowerment if you go through the planning of a lemonade stand business and make business decisions.

Entrepreneur

An entrepreneur is an individual who undertakes to supply a good or service to the market for profit. Entrepreneurs will usually invest their own capital in a business and take on the risks associated with the investment.

Once you invest some money and undertake to open up a lemonade stand business, you have become an entrepreneur.

Equal Pay

The requirement that men and women in the same employment must be paid at the same rate for like work or work rated as equal.

If you hire a boy or a girl to work the same job at your lemonade stand, you should pay them the same amount.

Equity

Equity is a beneficial interest in an asset.

If you work hard to develop or acquire assets and pay off the money borrowed to have these assets, you will be creating equity. Equity will help you to develop other businesses.

Exports

Goods or services sold to foreign countries.

If you were to bottle or can your lemonade and sell it to other countries, you would be exporting it.

Exit Strategy

This refers to the means by which, investors in a company realize all or part of their investment.

If you buy stock in a company you want to understand how, when and how much you will get back.

Family Life Cycle

The six stages of family life based on demographic data are:

1. Young single people
2. Young couples with no children
3. Young couples with youngest child under six years
4. Couples with dependent children
5. Older couples with no children at home
6. Older single people

These are helpful for marketers and advertisers marketing to these groups. Other groups evolve over time and it is important for you to understand groups that would be interested in your product and how and where you can connect with them.

Financier
A person who uses his or her own money to finance a business deal, venture or makes arrangements for such financing.

Focus Group
A focus group is an exploratory research group of participants led by a moderator, who meet for in-depth discussion on one particular topic or concept.

Forecasting
Estimating the future demand of goods and services by anticipating how buyers are likely to react under given sets of conditions.
You are forecasting when you sit down and try to estimate how many people will visit your stand and how much lemonade you will sell.

Fringe Benefits
Non-monetary benefits offered to the employees of a company in addition to their wages or salaries. They include company cars, expense accounts, the opportunity to buy company products at reduced prices, health care, social clubs etc.
If you give people who work for your stand a discount on the purchase of lemonade then you are offering them fringe benefits.

Gatekeeper
A gatekeeper in business is a manager in a large company who controls the flow of information.

General Meeting
A meeting that all the members of an association may attend.

Ghost Shopper
A ghost shopper is someone posing as a regular consumer, who is hired by a company who wants to know how their product is being sold at a store. Kind of like a shopping spy.

Golden Handcuffs
Financial incentives offered to key staff to persuade them to remain with an organization.

Green Marketing
Marketing products that benefit the environment. Better pollution controls and more energy-efficient production processes and product performance are part of green marketing.

Incentive
An incentive is a reason to buy a product. Providing you with a special reason to buy which is usually available for a limited period of time so that you buy at that point in time.

Initial Public Offering (IPO)
This refers to the process by which a company raises money, by issuing equity and gets listed on a stock exchange. This is when a company sells stock that can be bought and sold by many people. It is the dream of many people when they start businesses.

Impulse Buying
Impulse buying is the buying of a product by a consumer without previous intention and almost always without evaluation of competing brands.

Income
Any sum that a person or an organization receives either as a reward for effort or as a return on investments. The money you make (profit) on your lemonade stand business is income.

Industrial Espionage
Spying on a competitor to obtain trade secrets by dishonest means. The information sought often refers to the development of new products, manufacturing techniques, market information, upcoming advertising campaigns, research plans etc.

Industrial Relations
Industrial relations are the relationship between the management of an organization and its workforce. If industrial relations are good, the workforce will be well motivated to work hard for the benefit of the organization and its customers.

Innovation
Any new approach to designing, producing, or marketing goods that gives the innovator or the company an advantage over competitors. Some companies rely on bringing out new products based on established demand, while others develop technological innovations that open up new markets.

Insolvency
Insolvency is the inability to pay one's debts when they fall due. In the case of individuals this may lead to bankruptcy and in the case of companies to liquidation.

Insurance
A legal contract in which an insurer promises to pay a specified amount to another party, the insured, if a particular event (known as the peril) happens and the insured suffers a financial loss as a result. The insured has to pay an amount of money known as a premium for insurance.

Liquidity
Liquidity is the ability of an asset to be converted into cash as quickly as possible and without any reduction to its value.

Marketing
The process of planning and executing the conception, pricing, promotion and distribution of ideas, goods and services to create changes that satisfy individual and organizational objectives.
Marketing is an approach to doing business that focuses on identifying the customer's needs and preferences. Using this information, a company can shape the goods and services it provides, as well as the strategy it uses to bring these goods and services to the public, based on satisfying the customer.

Marketplace
A marketplace is a place where goods are offered for sale.

Market Share
Market share is the total number of units sold or dollars earned by one product or company in relation to the total number of products sold or dollars earned in an entire product class.

Money
Basically, money allows products and services to be exchanged. If you want to buy a product such as a music CD, it is the payment of money that completes the transaction and allows the ownership of the CD to be transferred to you.

Price
The price is the amount for which a thing is sold or can be bought at.

Quality Control
Quality control is the activities and techniques used to achieve and maintain a high standard of quality in a process. This procedure is concerned with finding and eliminating the causes of quality problems.

Seed Capital financing
The small amount of initial capital (money) required for the funding of research and development necessary before a company is set-up. The capital should enable a business plan to be drawn up.

Start-up Financing
This consists of capital provided to companies that have been in operation for less than one year, to facilitate all phases of bringing their products to market.

Trademark
This is the right of a seller to exclusive use of an identifying symbol or brand. For example, "e-Mentoring for Kids Program™" is trademarked. The "™" at the end of the phrase tells you that it is trademarked. There are laws to protect other people from using this trademarked phrase.

Target Market
This is the collection or population of customers or consumers that a company has in mind as the primary audience for its goods or services and to whom the company gears its marketing efforts to sell the good or service.

White Knight
This refers to a friendly acquirer sought by a company threatened by a less welcome buyer.

Closing Comments

Hopefully by now you have gone through this book and used the numerous ideas we have shared with you. You have put your imagination to work and come up with some amazing business ideas. You should feel wiser about business and confident that you have the talents and skills to further explore business.

Learning about business at an early age is not necessarily figuring out what you want to be when you grow-up. At this stage, business should be considered as an activity that is interesting and challenging. As you begin to understand business you will be well on your way in preparing for your future.

Sports, arts and music help you develop skills at an early age. Business skills can also be developed at an early age to help you manage your daily life and to prepare you for your working life. You have probably heard the expression, "If I knew what I know now" that people would do things differently and better. If you can learn some of the skills that you would normally learn later, you would do things so much better now and be better prepared for the future. Early skill development will give you a head start in business, make you more competitive and help you succeed.

Think of business skills as life skills that you can use every day as a kid. As you grow up you will realize that the sooner you develop these skills the better. Business skills cover a range of skills, which include reading, writing, time management, organizational skills, interpersonal skills (dealing with people) and many more. Please don't think of business skills solely as the obvious skills in a specific job. Everything you are able to do becomes a business skill and the more skills you have the more prepared you will be in your daily & business life.

You may find your career in one of the many responsibilities that are required to build a business. Take the time to explore some of these opportunities further. Once you have found an area of business that interests you, try and understand the skills that are required, and develop a plan for you to develop the needed skills.

Our DAB approach is hopefully something you will use on other business ideas. Please take time to apply this approach to develop other businesses that interest you, provide additional experience and develop your skills.
Good luck in your future and in your next business venture!

Printed in the United States
49233LVS00004B/1-8